Fourth Printing 1991

THE BLACK HISTORY TRIVIA QUIZ BOOK

MELVETT G. CHAMBERS

P.O. Box 390174
Denver, Colo. 80239
303-371-8729

THE BLACK HISTORY TRIVIA QUIZ BOOK, Copyright © 1990 by Melvett G. Chambers. All rights reserved. No part of this book may be used or reproduced in any manner, including photocopying, with out written permission from the publisher.

Fourth printing 1991
Third printing 1990 Revised
Second printing 1987
First printing 1986
Previous Edition Copyright © 1986

Book Design by: Melvett G. Chambers

Library of Congress Catalog Card Number 90-082410
ISBN 1-878807-12-9

Chambers, Melvett George
  The Black History Trivia Quiz Book

Printed in the United States of America

Published by: Melvett Chambers
              Author/Publisher
P.O. Box 390174
Denver, Colo. 80239

ACKNOWLEDGEMENT

I would like to express my gratitude to a number of people who contributed by giving material, advice and moral support. Without the help of many who shared, this book could have indeed been close to impossible, if not impossible to complete. To my private thanks I would like to add my public gratitude to: Inez Horton Doug and Wallace Yvonne McNair, Clay Worth and Dr. Irving Zelkind. For Strategic advice Quincy and Aundrey Wilkins. Thanks for being who and what you are, a very unique, caring and competent group of people. Finally I want to extend my appreciation to my best friend, Emma Chambers who participated in every aspect and phase of this book. I sincerely thank all these fine people.

PERMISSIONS ACKNOWLEDGMENTS

Stamp Designs Copyright© by: The United States Postal Service, Reproduced with Permission.

Denver Public Library, Western History Department. Photo's on pages; 68, 69, 70, 76, 79 and 80.

CONTENTS

Acknowledgements

Black Jockeys Who Won The Kentucky Derby
PAGE 1

Groups: Who Sang That Song
PAGE 2

The Black Screen
PAGE 3

Major Events in Black History 1526-1983
PAGE 6

Black Women in Music; Who Sang That Song
PAGE 12

Black Inventors and Scientists
PAGE 13

The Sports Scene # 1
PAGE 14

The Jazz Scene # 1
PAGE 17

Black First # 1
PAGE 19

True or False; Music
PAGE 25

Black First # 2
PAGE 27

The Jazz Scene # 2
PAGE 32

Rhythm and Blues; Who Sang That Song
PAGE 34

The Sports Scene # 2
PAGE 35

Real Names
PAGE 37

Black Heritage Stamps
PAGE 38

Black Congressmen of The Past
PAGE 45

Identify The Group
PAGE 49

Major Events in Black History # 2 1775-1983
PAGE 50

Black First # 3
PAGE 52

Nicknames; Sports
PAGE 54

Rhythm and Blues; Who Sang That Song # 2
PAGE 55

Inventions By Blacks; 1834-1950
PAGE 56

Black Writers
PAGE 63

Black Mayors; Past and Present
PAGE 65

Black Cowboys
PAGE 67

**Historic Landmarks
of Black Americans**
PAGE 72

Black Quotations
PAGE 81

Black Women
PAGE 84

**Rhythm and Blues;
Who Sang That Song**
PAGE 87

**Some Who Made
a Difference**
PAGE 90

**Who Sang
That Song "Sixties"**
PAGE 98

**The
Black Screen # 2**
PAGE 99

**Black Facts
At-a-Glance**
PAGE 108

Answers
PAGE 110

BLACK JOCKEYS, WHO WON THE KENTUCKY DERBY

From the time of the first running of the Kentucky Derby in 1875 until 1902, no less than 11 Black jockeys have won a total of 15 Kentucky Derbies in the history of the event. How may can you name.

	JOCKEY	MOUNT	YEAR
1	_____	Aristides	1875
2	_____	Baden Baden	1877
3	_____	Fonso	1880
4	_____	Apollo	1882
5	_____	Buchanan	1884
6	_____	Joe Cotton	1885
7	_____	Montrose	1887
8	_____	Riley	1890
9	_____	Kingman	1891
10	_____	Azra	1892
11	_____	Halma	1895
12	_____	Ben Brush	1896
13	_____	Plaudit	1898
14	_____	His Eminence	1901
15	_____	Alan-A-Dale	1902

GROUPS;
WHO SANG THAT SONG

Here are 15 big hits from the 60's, 70's and 80's by Black groups. Identify the group that sang each song. Write the number preceding the song alongside the group.

SONG		GROUP
1 "Aquarius"	_____	O'Jays
2 "Jump"	_____	Kool & the Gang
3 "Love Train"	_____	Ohio Players
4 "Celebration"	_____	Fifth Dimension
5 "I'll Be Around"	_____	Pointer Sisters
6 "Car Wash"	_____	Earth, Wind & Fire
7 "He's So Fine"	_____	Miracles
8 "A-B-C"	_____	Isley Brothers
9 "Great Pretender"	_____	Cameo
10 "Skin Tight"	_____	Kool & The Gang
11 "Shining Star"	_____	Platter's
12 "Shop Around"	_____	Jackson Five
13 "It's Your Thing"	_____	Chiffons
14 "Single Life"	_____	Rose Royce
15 "Emergency"	_____	Spinners

THE BLACK SCREEN
Films Featuring Black Actors

1. In 1972 Sidney Poitier made his directorial debut working on this Western in which he co-starred with Harry Belafonte and Ruby Dee. Name the movie.

2. Filmed entirely on location at the 1972 PUSH Expo in Chicago, this music documentary featured the finest Black talent working at the time. Name it.

3. Clevon Little stars as a Black sheriff sent to work in a racist town in a plot that ultimately backfired in the face of a corrupt state officer. Name the movie.

4. In 1974 Isaac Hayes stars as a fired police lieutenant who teams with a priest to solve a major ghetto murder. Name this film.

5. What one-time Muhammad Ali bodyguard played Clubber Lang in "Rocky III"?

6. She's the girl from Kansas in this 1979 musical, "The Wiz". Name the performer.

7. He was Diana Ross' main man in "Lady Sings The Blues" and also played in "The Empire Strikes Back".

8 He directed Richard Pryor and Gene Wilder in "Stir Crazy".

9 Name the movie based on the life of Muhammad Ali.

10 This Black actor won an Oscar for his portrayal of the sergeant in "An Officer and A Gentleman".

11 Brock Peters got his start playing tough characters as the evil Sergeant Brown in what movie?

12 Ethel Waters and Eddie Anderson headlined the all star cast of what movie?

13 Who was the actor whose voice emanated from Darth Vader's mask in "Star Wars"?

14 In 1958 Nat King Cole, Pearl Bailey, Cab Calloway, Ella Fitzgerald, Mahalia Jackson played in what movie?

15 In 1958 Sidney Poitier starred opposite Eartha Kitt in a story about the struggle for equality in Africa. Name the movie.

16 In 1968, the theme of this movie is injustice to a Black man hunted down following his escape from prison for a crime he did not commit. Name the movie.

17 Who was the director of the 1970 movie, "Watermelon Man"?

18 This movie was about a Black teacher (Sidney Poitier) who took a post in a tough London school and battles to reach rebellious youngsters. Name the movie.

19 In 1972 Motown Records entered the movie business with this film and won five Academy Award nominations. Name the film.

20 Diana Ross made her film debut as a singer in one of the most important film biographies about a Black woman, Billie Holiday. Name the film.

21 In "Some Kind of Hero" he played the Vietnam Vet trying to adjust to life in the United States.

22 Diana Ross portrays who in "Lady Sings The Blues"?

23 She supplied the voice of Big Mama in Disney's animated the "Fox and The Hound".

24 What film won Cicely Tyson an Academy Award nomination as best actress in 1973?

25 Who played the piano man in "Lady Sings The Blues"?

MAJOR EVENTS IN
BLACK HISTORY: 1526-1983

Without any doubt Black people figured importantly in many of the Spanish expeditions as well as in the successful English colonization that give birth to the United States of America. Listed below are some major events in Black History. How many of these can you answer correctly?

1. In 1983, Motwon Records celebrated its_____th Anniversary.

2. The first issue of Ebony Magazine was published by who?

3. She was appointed Brigadier General in the United States Army Nurses Corps in 1982.

4. He designed the Lunar Surface Ultraviolet Camera Spectrograph for Apollo 16.

5. People United to Save Humanity was organized in Chicago in 1971 by a former aide to Dr. Martin Luther King, Jr. Who was he?

6. The first Black person ever to be appointed to the United States Supreme Court was who?

   Thurgood Marshall

7. Who was the Black surgeon that perform the world's first open heart surgery?

8. Jan E. Matzeligner was the inventor of the lasting Machine which revolutionized what?

9. Who was the first Black baseball umpire in the Major Leagues?

10 She "Reached Out and Touched" thousands of listeners in a free Central Park concert in 1983. Who was she?

11 On October 14, 1834, Henry Blair of Maryland was granted a patent for what?

12 He was the first Black person to qualify for the 1975 Masters Golf Tournament.

13 The Brooklyn Excelsiors were the first Black professional what?

14 Who was the first Black accredited White House news correspondent?

15 The first coin honoring a Black American was a .50 cent piece of Booker T. Washington. When was it issued?

16 Charles Drew, Blood Plasma Researcher, served as Chief Surgeon of Freedmen's Hospital in what City?

17 He became the first Black football coach to reach 300 career victories. Name him.

18 1939, LaGuardia New York she is the first Black woman to be appointed a judge.

19 Cambridge Massachusetts 1894 he became the first Black person to be awarded a Ph.D. by Harvard.

20 In 1935, a Black chemist develops Physostigmine, a drug for treatment of Glaucoma. Name him.

21 1954, this decision by the U.S. Supreme Court declared segregation in public schools to be unconstitutional.

22 March 17, 1865, Aaron Anderson wins Navy Medal of Honor for heroic action aboard the USS, what?

23 1949, he was the first Black pilot in the U.S. Naval Reserve. Name him.

24 The first Black woman lawyer received her degree from Howard University, School of Law in Washington, D.C., in 1872. Name her.

25 January 25, 1966 she became the first Black woman named to a Federal judgeship.

26 He was an educator and founder of Tuskegee Institute.

27 In 1897, Andrew J. Beard received $50,000 for an invention called what?

28 Both the gas mask and the traffic light were invented by who?

29 Who developed the preserving technique for blood transfusions?

30 In September, 1960 she won 3 gold medals in Olympic competition.

31 What Black female won both the Wimbledon and U.S. Championships in tennis, in 1957 and 1958?

32 1526, the first group of Black people to set foot on what is now the United States, are brought by a Spanish explorer to where?

33 The first issue of Ebony Magazine sold how many copies?

34 In 1962 he became the first Black American to command a U.S. Warship, the USS Falgout. Who is he?

35 1538 Estevanico, a Black explorer is credited with the discovery of what is now Arizona and

36 What month, date and year did Richard Theodore Greener graduate from Harvard?

37 Who was the first Black American elected to Congress from the East?

38 The first Black woman Legislator elected to Pennsylvania Legislature was whom?

39 Who was the first Black President of Georgetown University in Washignton, D.C.?

40 The first Black newspaper "Freedom's Journal" was published When?

41 Booker T. Washington was born a slave in what state?

42 What year was the Bethel African Methodist Episcopal Church founded?

43 What date did Congress pass the Civil Rights Bill?

44 Who was the first Black person to enroll in the University of Tennessee?

45 He was the first Black golfer to win admission to the Professional Golfer's Association.

46 The first Black newspaper in the South, "The Colored American" was published in Augusta, Georgia and edited by who?

47 The USS Harmon became the first fighting ship of the U.S. named after a Black man. Name him.

48 The first Black person to be appointed a chaplain in the U.S. Army was who?

49 What Black person was nominated for vice president at the 1968 Democratic National Convention?

50 She is founder and chief executive of the Saint Luke Penny Savings Bank in Richmond, Virginia 1903.

BLACK WOMEN IN MUSIC; WHO SANG THAT SONG

Here are rock'n'roll top hits from the 1960s' song by Black women groups who were an integral part of rock'n'roll during the 60s'. Write the number preceding the song alongside the group.

SONG   **GROUP**

1 "Maybe"   _____ Martha & The Vandellas

2 "Dedicated To The One I Love"   _____ Supremes

3 "He's a Rebel"   _____ The Chantels

4 "Please Mr Postman"   _____ Dixie Cups

5 "Wah Wahtusi"   _____ The Cookies

6 "Love is Here and Now You're Gone"   _____ The Blue-Belles

7 "Nowhere To Run"   _____ The Marvelettes

8 "I Sold My Heart To The Junkman"   _____ The Crystals

9 "Don't Say Nothing Bad About My Baby"   _____ Orlons

10 "Chapel of Love"   _____ The Shirelles

BLACK INVENTORS AND SCIENTISTS

listed below are the names of some notable Black inventors and scientists. Write the number preceding their names alongside their profession and birth date.

NAME		PROFESSION
1	Andrew J. Beard	_____ Inventor 1850-1910
2	Henry Blair	_____ Engineer 1887-1958
3	David Crosthwail, Jr	_____ Surgeon 1885-1961
4	Elijah McCoy	_____ Technician 1892-1961
5	Lewis Temple	_____ Inventor 1800-1854
6	George Washington Carver	_____ Blood Plasama Researcher 1904-50
7	Norbert Rillieux	_____ Inventor 1877-1963
8	Frederick McKinley Jones	_____ Inventor, Draftsman, Engineer 1848-1928
9	Lewis Howard Latimer	_____ Medical Scientist 1883-1959
10	Ernest E. Just	_____ Engineer 1898
11	Charles Drew	_____ Biologist 1883-1941
12	Garrett A. Morgan	_____ Inventor 1806-1894
13	Archie Alexander	_____ Inventor 1844-1928
14	Ulysses Grant Dailey	_____ Agricultural Scientist 1864-1943
15	Williams A. Hinton	_____ Inventor 1804-1860

THE SPORTS SCENE #1

Outstanding amateur and professional Black athletes, in baseball, basketball, boxing, football, tennis, golf, track and field. See how many of these you can correctly identify.

1. He was the oldest man to hold a world boxing title at age 44.

2. Who fought Muhammad Ali in the Thrilla in Manila?

3. Name the first Black to win the U.S. Men's National Tennis title.

4. This basketball player scored 100 points in a single game, March 2, 1962.

5. In 1967, he was stripped of his heavyweight boxing title. Name him. *Muhammad Ali*

6. Who won the light-heavyweight boxing Gold Medal in the 1960 Olympics?

7. Who hit three home runs in the final game of the 1977 World Series. *Reggie Jackson*

8. He was known as the Louisville Lip.

9. Muhammad Ali beat this boxer to become World Heavyweight champion for the first time.

10. Who retired from major league baseball with 755 home runs to his credit?

14

11 What Olympic track star was nicknamed "The Ebony Express"?

12 Who was the first boxer to hold the World Heavyweight championship three times?

13 Who won the fight of the Century on March 8, 1971?

14 He was named football back of the decade from 1950 to 1960.

15 What football player rushed for 2,003 yards in 1973?

16 This light-heavyweight boxer was known as "The Mongoose".

17 When did Joe Louis retire?

18 How long did Joe Louis hold the Heavyweight boxing title?

19 In 1974 Lou Brock stole 118 bases and broke who's record?

20 Ernie Banks won national league player M.V.P. award back to back in?

21 In September 1960, she won 3 gold medals in Olympic competition.

22 What years did Roy Campanella win baseball's Most Valuable Players award?

23 Who won the 1976 Olympic boxing gold medal in the light-welterweight division?

24 He was named the 1980-81 NBA Player of the year.

25 This 7 foot Nigerian center led the University of Houston Cougars to a 31-3 record in 1982.

THE JAZZ SCENE #1

Listed below are the names and birth dates of some outstanding Black Jazz Artists. Identify the instrument that they each play.

	NAME	DATE	INSTRUMENT
1	Herbie Hancock	1940	
2	Freddie Hubbard	1938	
3	Anthony Williams	1945	
4	Larry Young	1940	
5	Yusef Lateef	1921	
6	Nat Adderley	1931	
7	Jimmy Cobb	1929	
8	Ted Curson	1935	
9	Eddie Harns	1934	
10	Teddy Edwards	1924	
11	Donald Byrd	1932	
12	Ron Carter	1937	
13	Don Cherry	1936	
14	Hank Crawford	1934	
15	Grant Green	1911	
16	Ramsey Lewis	1935	
17	Reggie Workman	1937	

18	John Tehical	1936	_____
19	Stanley Turrentine	1934	_____
20	Archie Shepp	1937	_____
21	Shirley Scott	1934	_____
22	Jimmy Owens	1943	_____
23	Paul Humphrey	1935	_____
24	Phil Woods	1931	_____
25	Les McCann	1935	_____

BLACK FIRST #1

The following list describes a wide spectrum of pioneering events in Black American History, such as the first group of Blacks to set foot on what is now the United States in 1526, to the first Black to win a world boxing title in 1890.

1 Born a slave in Philadelphia in 1762, he became the first Black physician in the United States in 1783. Who was he?

2 This Black jockey rode Aristides to victory in the first running of the 1875 Kentucky Derby.

3 In 1861, the first Black person wounded in the Civil War was 65 years old.

4 In 1845, the first Black lawyer to be formally admitted to the bar was who?

5 In 1621 he became the first Black child born in the American Colonies. Who was he?

6 The first Black college graduate received his degree from Bowdoin College in Maine, in 1826. Who was he?

7 September 21, 1872, he was the first Black person to be admitted to the U.S. Naval Academy.

8 June 15, 1877 he was the first Black person to graduate from West Point. Who was he?

9 1884 he becomes the first Black Major League baseball player for Toledo in the American Association.

10 The first Black director of physical education, was Molineaux Hewlett who taught at what university?

11 Henry O. Flipper was the first Black graduate of what military academy?

12 P.B.S. Pinchback became the first Black Governor of what State on December 9, 1872?

13 In 1790 according to the first census, there were how many Black people in the United States?

14 He was the first Black person elected to the State Supreme Court of South Carolina, February 18, 1885

15 October 28, 1862 the first official all Black unit in the Civil War, fights a victorious skirmish where?

16 In 1884 the first Black baseball team, the Cuban Giants was formed in New York City by who?

17 In 1866 they were the first Black State Representatives to sit in any State Legislature. Name them.

18 In 1885 he was the first Black State Legislator to represent a constituency in which the majority were White.

19 In 1943 the first Liberty Ship, named after a Black American is launched from a New Jersey shipyard to begin its career of carrying war cargo to Europe during World War II. Name that person.

20 Records at the medical college of the New York Infirmary indicate that she was the first Black woman physician in the United States from 1872-1881.

21 He became the first Black person to preside over a national political convention, becoming temporary chairman of the Republican Party's National Convention in 1884.

22 Name the first hospital for Black people in the United States to be granted a charter.

23 The first group of Black people to set foot on what is now the United States were brought by a Spanish explorer to where?

24 The first show that featured Black female singers was produced where?

25 Name the first independent republic in Africa in 1847.

26 The first Black person to graduate from Harvard university in 1870 was who?

27 December 25, 1863 Robert Blake wins Navy Medal of Honor for distinguished service aboard what?

28 Sojourner Truth was born about 1797, her birth name was what?

29 Name the first Black Lieutenant Governor of Louisiana in 1868?

30 Who was the first Black person to be elected to public office in 1836?

31 Who led the first major revolt against slavery in 1831?

32 1863 he is appointed surgeon of the 17th Regiment, is said to be the first commissioned Black medical officer.

33 In 1865 he became the first Black minister to deliver a sermon in the House of Representatives.

34 A Black furtrapper established the first permanent settlement at what was to become Chicago. Who was he?

35 In 1786 he served in the Revolution as a Minuteman. Became the first Black minister with a White congregation.

36 1795 the first Black missionary minister to work with Indians was?

37 The first Black person to win the Congressional Medal of Honor was?

38 In 1770 her first poem was printed under the title "A Poem by Phillis". Who was she?

39 In 1846 America's first Black studio artist, painted the William Berthelet portrait. Name him.

40 In 1865 America's first Black newspaper in the South "The Colored American", is published in Augusta, Georgia and edited by Who?

41 1853 the first novel written by a Black person and published is a work of?

42 1873 the first Black municipal judge is elected in Little Rock Arkansas. Who was he?

43 The first coin honoring a Black person was a .50 cent piece, which bears a relief bust of who?

44 May 1965 she was named ambassador to Luxembourg, to become the first Black woman ambassador. Who was she?

45 October 14, 1834 the first Black person to obtain a patent from the United States Patent Office was?

46 January, 1955 she was the first Black woman to sing with the Metropolitan Opera Company.

47 In 1892 the first Black college football game was played between?

48 1865 the first Black newspaper in the South was the?

49 In 1862 she becomes the first Black woman in the United States to earn an M.A. degree.

50 In 1865, in New Orleans the first Convention of Black Newspaper men met and out of it came what?

TRUE OR FALSE; MUSIC

Here are some statements about Black singing groups and their lead singer. Write the letter "T" next to those statements that are true and the letter "F" next to those that are false.

1 _____ Eddie Kendricks had formely been a member of the Temptations.

2 _____ Curtis Mayfield was the lead singer for the Miracles.

3 _____ In 1976 "Love Machine" was a # 1 hit song for the Miracles.

4 _____ James Brown's backing group, are the Famous Flames.

5 _____ Deniece Williams was a former member of Stevie Wonder's backing group called Wonderlove.

6 _____ Singer Clyde McPhatter was the lead singer for the Drifters.

7 _____ The Marvelettes sang the hit "Come and Get These Memories".

8 _____ The original name of the Supremes was the Primettes.

9 _____ The jazz giant of the 60's, who had an electronic disco hit in 1983 with "Rockit" was George Duke.

10 _____   Smokey Robinson was the lead singer for the Miracles.

11 _____   Lionel Richie was once the lead singer for the Commodores.

12 _____   Otis Redding, Sam Cooke and Jimi Hendrix all died tragically before turning 30.

13 _____   In 1983 Harold Melvin and the Blue Notes called it quits.

14 _____   Hank Ballard wrote the hit song "twist".

15 _____   Melvin Franklin, David Ruffin, Paul Williams and Eddie Kendricks were all members of the Temptations.

BLACK FIRST #2

1. Who was the first Black woman elected to the U.S. Congress?

2. Who was the first Black Judge of a U.S. Circuit Court of Appeals?

3. Who was the first Black General in the Army?

4. Name the first Black American to become a Roman Catholic Bishop.

5. Who was America's first Black woman millionaire?

6. Who was the first Black Four Star General?

7. Who was the first Black contestant in the Miss America Pageant?

8. He was America's first Black scientist, and helped plan Washington, D.C.

9. Who was the first Black to be honored on a postage stamp?

10. Who was the first Black leader to be honored with an American National Holiday?

11. In 1945, she was the first Black nurse to be commissioned in the Navy Reserve Corps.

12. In 1926 she was the first Black woman lawyer to practice before the U.S. Supreme Court.

13 He was the first Black Bishop of the Episcopal Church.

14 Who was the first Black "Mr. America"?

15 In 1975, he became the first Black man to manage a major league baseball team.

16 Who was the first member of the National Track and Field Hall of Fame when it opened in 1978?

17 In 1945 he became the first Black person appointed a Judge of the Custom's Court.

18 She was the first Black woman to publish a novel, "Lola Leary" The Shadows.

19 In 1948, he became the first Black commissioned officer in the regular U.S. Marine Corps.

20 Who was the organizer and first bishop of the African Methodist Episcopal Church?

21 Who was the first Black major league baseball captain?

22 He became the first Black to play in the Master's Golf Tournament.

23 What is the name of the first Black post season bowl football game?

24 1919, he became the first Black to play professional football.

25 Who was the first Black baseball player to win the leagues most valuable players award?

26 In 1947, he became the first Black pitcher in the major leagues for the Brooklyn Dodgers.

27 He was the first Black pitcher in the American League in 1948.

28 He was the first Black person to perform in the Ziegfeld Follies.

29 Who was the first Black person to star in a regular dramatic T.V. series?

30 Who was the first Black person to win an Oscar in 1940?

31 Her first book was poetry titled, "Once" published in 1968. What is her name?

32 The first Black actor to win an Academy Award was who?

33 Name the first Black entertainer to host a daytime game show.

34 Name the first movie with an all Black cast.

35 Who was the first Black person named director of an American orchestra (The Newark based New Jersey Symphony)?

36 In 1951 she became the first Black woman to dance for the Metropolitan Opera in New York.

37 Who was the first Black musician to play for the Philadelphia Orchestra during the 1970-71 season?

38 He was the host of the first televised Miss Black America Pageant in 1977.

39 Who was the first Black man to win an Oscar?

40 Who was the first Black Woman to appear on the cover of Vogue Magazine?

41 What is the name of the first Black Sorority?

42 December 3, 1874, Frederick Douglass published the first issue of his newspaper. What was the name of it?

43 Who was the first Black United States Senator (1870-71) from mississippi?

44 Who was the first Black to serve a full term (1875-1881) in the U.S. Senate?

45 The first Black daily newspaper in the United States, was what?

46 In 1982, he became the second Black Four-Star General in the United States Army.

47 In 1970, he became the first Black person to hold a seat on the New York Stock Exchange.

48 The first Black President of Fisk University was who?

49 Who was the first Black person to win a Nobel Prize?

50 In 1949 he became the first person to graduate from the Naval Academy at Annapolis.

JAZZ SCENE #2

Listed below are the names of some outstanding Black jazz artists. Identify the instrument that they each play.

	NAME	INSTRUMENT
1	Cannonball Adderley	_____
2	Herschel Evans	_____
3	Pete Johnson	_____
4	Bud Scott	_____
5	Johnny St. Cyr	_____
6	Walter Page	_____
7	Jack Washington	_____
8	Mutt Carey	_____
9	Sidney Catlett	_____
10	Jimmy Harrison	_____
11	Tubby Hall	_____
12	Sidney DeParis	_____
13	Johnny Dodds	_____
14	Baby Dodds	_____
15	Jay C. Higginbotham	_____
16	Keg Johnson	_____
17	Lonnie Johnson	_____

18 John Kirby _____

19 Tommy Ladnier _____

20 Meade Lux Lewis _____

21 John Lindsay _____

22 William F. Newton _____

23 Jimmy Noone _____

24 Tricky Sam Naton _____

25 Lee Morgan _____

RHYTHM AND BLUES; WHO SANG THAT SONG

Here are 10 top Rhythm and Blues, songs from 1972-73 by Black singers. Identify the singer of each song.

SONG **SINGER**

1 "Ben" _____

2 "Superfly" _____

3 "Funky Worm" _____

4 "Papa Was a Rollin Stone" _____

5 "Superstition" _____

6 "Boogie Down" _____

7 "My Ding-A-Ling" _____

8 "Power of Love" _____

9 "Do Your Thing" _____

10 "Love Train" _____

THE SPORTS SCENE #2

Outstanding amateur and professional Black athletes, in baseball, basketball, boxing, football, tennis, golf, track and field.

1 This basball player was known as the Say-Hey-Kid.
   a. Willie Mays
   b. Frank Robinson
   c. Hank Aaron
   d. Maury Wills

2 Muhammad Ali beat this boxer to become World Heavyweight Champion for the first time.
   a. Joe Frazier
   b. Jack Johnson
   c. Sonny Liston
   d. Larry Holmes

3 Who won the 1973 Heavyweight Title from Joe Frazier?
   a. George Foreman
   b. Jimmy Ellis
   c. Muhammad Ali
   d. Ken Norton

4 Name the first Black person to win a Wimbledon Singles' in 1957.
   a. Arthur Ashe
   b. Althea Gibson
   c. Fritz Pollard
   d. Paul Cuffee

5 In 1947 he became the first Black pitcher in the Major Leagues, for the Brooklyn Dodgers.
   a. Satchell Paige
   b. Dan Bankhead
   c. Mike Norris
   d. Reggie Jackson

6 Ernie Banks won the National League Players MVP Award back-to-back in:
   a. 1958-59
   b. 1957-58
   c. 1959-60
   d. 1962-63

7 Who was the Black baseball player that broke Babe Ruth's record of most home runs in a World Series.
    a. Reggie Jackson   c. Willie Mays
    b. Hank Aaron   d. Bob Gibson

8 Larry Holmes defended his World Boxing Council Heavyweight Title how many times in 1981?
    a. 10   c. 0
    b. 3   d. 5

9 He won the 1976 Olympic Boxing Gold Medal in the light welterweight division.
    a. Sugar Ray Leonard   c. Marvin Hagler
    b. Floyd Patterson   d. Michael Spinks

10 Henry Armstrong was inducted into the Black Athletes Hall of Fame in:
    a. 1975   c. 1970
    b. 1980   d. 1968

REAL NAMES

You probably know these Black leaders by the names listed here, but these aren't their birth names. See how many you can get correct, write the birth name in the blank space alongside the present name.

NAME	BIRTH NAME
1 Soujourner Truth	_____
2 Sugar Ray Robinson	_____
3 Ray Charles	_____
4 Martin Luther King, Jr.	_____
5 B.B. King	_____
6 Jackie "Mom's" Mabley	_____
7 Mr. T	_____
8 Muhammad Ali	_____
9 Kareem Abdul Jabbar	_____
10 Chubby Checker	_____
11 Bobby "Blue" Bland	_____
12 Chuck Berry	_____
13 Stevie Wonder	_____
14 W.E.B. Dubois	_____
15 Joe Louis	_____

BLACK HERITAGE STAMPS

Among the many commemorative stamps issued by the United States Postal Service, are the on going Black Heritage United States of America series of stamps. Since 1978, a new stamp has appeared in this series each year. Each stamp marks the achievements of a Black American whose accomplishments have enriched our society.

1 Carter G. Woodson, Black historian, born in 1875, the son of a poor family of former slaves. Despite his poverty and few educational opportunities open to Blacks at the time, he went on to become one of the most respected historians, best known for his 35 years as editor of the "Journal of Negro History". He brought standards of excellence to his research, writing and teaching that has influenced the study of Black History ever since. **What was the month, date and year that the Carter G. Woodson stamp was issued?**

© U.S. Postal Service

2 Sojourner Truth, abolitionist; born Isabel Baumfree in Hurley, N.Y., 1797. She became the first outstanding Afro-American woman to speak out publicly against slavery. A champion of women's rights, Truth attended the second National Woman's Suffrage Convention, held 1852 in Akron, Ohio. Here she made her famous "Ain't I A Woman" speech.
What was the month, date and year that the Sojourner Truth stamp was issued?

© U.S. Postal service

3 Mary Mcleod Bethune, educator, civic leader; born near Mayesville SC 1875. She attend Scotia College in North Carolina 1888-95, and the Moody Bible Institute in Chicago 1895-97. Bethune opened a school in Daytona, Fl for Black children, that provided vocational and academic training at the primary and secondary levels. The school ultimately evoled into Bethume-Cookman College. U. S. Presidents Calvin Coolidge, Herbert Hoover and Harry S. Truman appointed her to various government post. She served as Franklin D. Roosevelt's special advisor on Minority Affairs 1935-44 and as director of National Youth Administrations Division of Negro Affairs 1936-44. The latter appoinment made her the first Black woman to head a federal agency division.

© U.S. Postal Service

What was the month, date and year that the Mary McLeod Bethune stamp was issued?

4 Benjamin Banneker, mathematician scientist, born in Ellicott Mills, MD 1731. Banneker received his early schooling from a Quaker family. He gained notice after he accurately predicted the solar eclipse that occurred in 1789. In that same year he was appointed a member of the surveying team that set the boundaries of Washington D.C.
What was the month, date and year that the Benjamin Banneker stamp was issued?

© U.S. Postal Service

5 Martin Luther King, Jr., born in Atlanta GA 1929. He organized and led the first mass Civil Rights movement in the history of the United States. Dr. King was able to gather active support from both Blacks and Whites for his program of non-violent protest against discrimination and segregation. Dr. King's 1963 march on Washington D.C. brought 200,000 peaceful demonstrators to the steps of the Lincoln Memorial. In 1964, he was awarded the Nobel peace Prize. Dr. Martin L King Jr. was tragically slain in Memphis Tennessee on April 4, 1968.
What was the month, date and year that the Martin Luther King, Jr. stamp was issued?

©U.S. Postal Service

6 Harriet Tubman, born into slavery in Maryland, around 1820. In 1849, she escaped to the North by the "Underground Railroad", a secret network designed to help fugitive slaves. Once she was free, she decided to risk her own freedom by returning to the South to help other Blacks escape. Between 1850 and the outbreak of the Civil War, she made the dangerous journey into the South some 19 times. During the War she served in the Union Army both as a scout and a spy behind Confederate lines. **What was the month, date and year that the Harriet Tubman stamp was issued?**

©U.S. Postal Service

7 Jean Baptiste Pointe DuSable, pioneer, entrepreneur. Place of birth has been listed as Santo Domingo, Haiti and French, Canada. He established trading posts on the sites of the present cities of Michigan City; Indiana; Peoria, Illinois and Huron, Michigan. Of all the trading posts, the most important post was on the site of Chicago, Illinois. This was the site where he constructed a log home for his wife and family on. It is recognized as the first settlement of Chicago.
What was the month, date and year that the Jean Baptiste Pointe DuSable stamp was issued?

© U.S. Postal Service

8 Jackie Robinson, born 1919, in Cairo, GA. He received an athletic scholarship to UCLA, where he excelled in four varsity sports. In 1945, he broke the color barrier in baseball minor leagues when he was signed to play for the Montreal Royals. his success with the Royals led to his signing with the Brooklyn Dodgers in 1947, when he became the first Black to play in the major leagues. Because Jackie Robinson took that first step, all professional sports were eventually opened to Black athletes.
What was the month, date and year that the Jackie Robinson stamp was issued?

© U.S. Postal Service

9 Whitney Moore Young Jr. Civil Rights leader, born in Lincoln Ridge, KY 1921. Whitney Young served from 1961 until his death in 1971, as the executive director of the National Urban League. As a consultant to President Lyndon B. Johnson on racial matters. He strongly influenced the federal anti-poverty programs of the 1960s.
What was the month, date and year that the Whitney Moore Young, Jr stamp was issued?

© U.S. Postal Service

10 James Weldon Johnson, born 1871 in Jacksonville, Florida, educated at Columbia and Atlanta Universities. From 1916 to 1930, he played a key role in policy making of the NAACP and eventually became executive secretary. Johnson is most often remembered for writing the lyrics for "Lift Every Voice and Sing". The poem is often referred to as the Black national anthem.
What was the month, date and year that the James Weldon Johnson stamp was issued?

© U.S. Postal Service

11 Scott Joplin composer, pianist. Born in Texarkana, Texas 1868. The music called "Ragtime" was America's most popular music during the early 20th Century and its most famous composer was the "King of Ragtime" Scott Joplin. He was one of the greatest innovators in the history of American music. In 1976 Joplin was awarded the Pulitzer Prize, after his death for his ragtime opera "Treemonisha", composed 60 years earlier. **What was the month, date and year that the Scott Joplin stamp was issued?**

©U.S. Postal Service

12 Ida B. Wells, Civil-rights advocate, teacher and journalist. She wrote articles about second-rate education given to Blacks in segregated city schools and publicized lynchings. In her crusade against lynchings, she lectured in Great Britain and found anti-lynching and anti-segregation societies. She encouraged women to form civic clubs. She became the first woman probation officer in Chicago courts. Wells devoted her life to fighting racism and for social justice. **What was the month, date and year that the Ida B. Wells stamp was issued?**

©U.S. Postal Service

43

13 A. Phillip Randolph, Black labor leader born in Crescent City, Florida, April 1889. A pullman porter, founder of the "Brotherhood", of sleepy car porters, he used his position as editor of a magazine, "The Messenger", to become the voice of the Brotherhood, educating Black porters and the community. Randolph was very influential on the national level and showed his leadership when he organized the "March-on-Washington Movement", to involve some 100,000 Blacks. The march was canceled when President Roosevelt signed Executive Order 8802, a week prior to the date of the march. A Fair Employment Practices Committee was established to enforce the Order. The Order forbade discrimination in government and defense job hiring. Discrimination was reduced, setting a precedent for ensuing governmental action against employment barriers. Randolph stuided labor economics in two New York colleges, which attributes to his success as a Black labor and Civil Rights leader for more than 50 years. **What was the month, date and year that the A. Phillip Randolph stamp was issued?**

©U.S. Postal Service

BLACK CONGRESSMEN OF THE PAST

This political tradition was started more than a century ago by Joseph H. Rainey, the first Black Congressman in the House of Representatives, and Hiram R. Revels, the first Black Congressman to serve in the U.S. Senate. Here are fifteen Black Congressmen from the past, see how many you can identify.

1. U.S. Senator from Mississippi (1875-1881), born a slave in Farmville, Prince Edward County Virgainia on March 1, 1841. Named Register of the U.S. Treasury Department by President James A. Garfield. Who was he?

2. Born a slave in 1840 near Warrenton, North Carolina. In 1868 participated in the Constitutional Convention of North Carolina, was selected to the State Legislature and served for six years. United States Congress man from North Carolina (1875-1877). Who was he?

3. U.S. Congressman from Alabama (1875-1877), at one time, he was considered the most influential Black in Alabama, was born a slave in Muscogee County, Georgia in 1846. Spent his last days in Colorado where he was killed in a hunting mishap. Who was this Congressman?

4. U.S. Congressman from Illinois (1934-1942). The first Black Democrat ever elected to the Congress. Born near Lafayette in Chambers County, Alabama, on December 22, 1883. Left home at age fourteen, earned his way through school by working on a farm as an office boy to Tuskegge's President, Booker T. Washington. Attended Columbia University in New York briefly and studied law, qualified for the bar and started his practice in Washington. Who was he?

5 U.S. Senator from Mississippi (1870-1871). A native of North Carolona, was the first Black person to serve in the U.S. Senate. Born 1822, educated in Indiana, and attended Knox College in Illinois. Ordained a minister in the African Methodist Church. After leaving the Senate, he was named President of Alcorn University near Lorman, Mississippi. Who was he?

6 U.S. Congressman from South Carolina (1869-1879). The first Black Congressman in the House of Representatives, born in 1832 in Georgetown, South Carolina. Upon his retirement from politics, he was appointed a special agent for the U.S. Treasury Department in Washington, D.C. Who was he?

7 U.S. Congressman from Mississippi (1873-1877; 1881-1883). The first Black American to preside over a national convention of the Republican party, elected to the House of Representatives in 1873, 1875 and 1881. In 1869 he was named a justice of the peace for Adams County, and elected to the Mississippi State Legislature. During his later years, he wrote two books: "The Facts of the Reconstruction" and "Some Historical Errors of James Ford Rhodes". Who was he?

8 U.S. Congressman from Louisiana (1875-1877). Born 1844 in Louisiana, earned his living as a bricklayer, until his enlistment in the Union Army in 1863. Lost a leg during the storming of Fort Blakely. After his discharge from the Army, as a Sergeant-Major, he was named U.S. Inspector of Customs for Louisiana. Died in 1913. Who was he?

9 U.S. Congressman from South Carolina (1871-1873). Born a slave in 1842 in Aiken, South Carolina. Was a successful farmer, served two years in the State Legislature before being elected to Congress. In 1873 was appointed a magistrate in the city of Charleston. Who was he?

10 U.S. Congressman from Illinois (1929-1935). Was the first Black American to win a seat in the U.S. House of Representatives in the 20th Century, and the first to be elected from a Northern State. Born in Florence, Alabama. In Chicago, he amassed a fortune in real estate and the stock market. In 1904 entered politics successfully when he was elected Cook County Commissioner. Who was he?

11 U.S. Congressman from North Carolina (1889-1893). He was born in Henderson, North Carolina in 1857. He received his B.A. and M. A. degrees from Shaw University and later studied law. Served two terms in the House of Representatives. Who was he?

12 U.S. Congressman from South Carolina (1873-1875; 1877-1879). Was born in 1825 in Greenbriar County, Virginia of free parents. At the age of 19 he became a preacher in Missouri for the Methodist Episcopal Church. Upon his retirement from public life in 1880, he was named African Methodist Episcopal Bishop of the Texas and Louisiana Conference and became President of Paul Quinn College in Waco, Texas. Who was he?

13 U.S. Congressman from Illinois (1970-1972). Had a brief, tragic career in Congress. Elected from the Seventh District (Chicago West Side) in 1970 and re-elected in 1972. Died in an airplane crash in December. Following his death, he was succeeded by his wife, Cardiss, who won a special election in 1973. Who was he?

14 U.S. Congressman from Illinois (1943-1971). He represented the First Congressional District of Illinois for 28 years. A native of Albany, Georgia, Chairman of the Democratic National Committee, became the first Black American to be elected its Vice Chairman. Who was he?

15 U.S. Congressman from New York (1945-1971). Was a legend in his time and one of the most controversial figures to grace American Politics. During the 50's he emerged as Congress's leading Black spokesman and for six years was the powerful Chairman of the House Education and Labor Committee. Who was he?

IDENTIFY THE GROUP

Here are the names of 15 singers who sang with very popular groups. How many of these groups can you identify and match with the singer.

	SINGER	GROUP
1	Chaka Khan	_____
2	Philippe Wynne	_____
3	Lionel Richie	_____
4	Maurice White	_____
5	David Ruffin	_____
6	Eddie Kendricks	_____
7	Curtis Mayfield	_____
8	Diana Ross	_____
9	Melvin Franklin	_____
10	Smokey Robinson	_____
11	Harold Melvin	_____
12	Paul Williams	_____
13	Michael Jackson	_____
14	Clyde McPhatter	_____
15	Peter Tosh	_____

MAJOR EVENTS IN BLACK HISTORY #2 1775-1983

Here are some major events in Black History. Write the letter "T" next to those statements that are true and the letter "F" next to those that are false.

1. _____ November 1, 1945 the first issue of Ebony Magazine was published.

2. _____ Charles Young, the third Black person to be admitted to the U.S. Military Academy at West Point, graduated in 1889.

3. _____ James A. Hearly was consecrated Bishop of Portland, Maine in 1875.

4. _____ Jackie Robinson and Roy Campanella were the first Black men to play on mixed baseball teams in the South.

5. _____ At the battle of Bunker Hill, in 1775 Peter Salem became a hero when he shot British Major Pitcairn.

6. _____ By 1983, there were 1,000 Black female Officers in the services.

7. _____ George Washington Carver received a degree in Agricultural Science in 1905.

8. _____ Roy Wilson became the first Black student to enter the University of Mississippi.

9. _____ Former President Carter appointed Andrew Young as U.S. Ambassador to the United Nations.

10 _____ Lloyd August Hall, chemist discovered Curing Salts for the preserving and processing of meats.

11 _____ Lake Erie 1813, 10 to 25% of Admiral Perry's victorious force in Naval battle with the British were Black Americans.

12 _____ 1900 John H. Alexander graduated from West Point.

13 _____ December 25, 1776 two Black Americans, Prince Whipple and Oliver Cromwell cross the Delaware with Washington.

14 _____ The first Transcontinental flight by Black civilian pilots were made by Charles Alfred Anderson and Albert Ernest Forsythe.

15 _____ In 1872 Alcon College became the first Black land grant college.

BLACK FIRST #3

1. In 1960 he became the first Boxer in history to regain the heavyweight title.
   - a. Sugar Ray Robinson
   - b. Sonny Liston
   - c. Floyd patterson
   - d. Muhammad Ali

2. Who was the first Black contestant in the Miss America Pageant?
   - a. Cheryl A. Browne
   - b. Patricia Harris
   - c. Janet Collins
   - d. Leslie Uggams

3. The first issue of Ebony Magazine was published by
   - a. Walter White
   - b. John Williams
   - c. John H. Johnson
   - d. James A Bland

4. Who was elected the first Black Congressman from the East?
   - a. Frederick Douglass
   - b. Adam Clayton Powell
   - c. Hiram R. Revels
   - d. Richard Allen

5. Who was the first Black woman elected to the U.S. Congress?
   - a. Mary Patterson
   - b. Sara Boone
   - c. Shirley Chishoim
   - d. Lena Walker

6. Who was the first Black Major League baseball captain?
   - a. Willie Mays
   - b. Hank Aaron
   - c. Frank Robinson
   - d. Maury Wills

7. Who was the first Black baseball player to play in Major League baseball?
   - a. Jackie Robinson
   - b. Roy Campanella
   - c. Frank Robinson
   - d. Willie Mays

8 What city did the first Black Catholic Bishop hold his post?
  a. Boston
  b. Atlanta
  c. Memphis
  d. Baltimore

9 Who was the first Black person to star in a regular dramatic T.V. series?
  a. Bill Cosby
  b. Sammy Davis, Jr.
  c. Sidney Poitier
  d. Richard Pryor

10 Who was the Black surgeon that performed the world's first open heart surgery?
  a. Daniel H. Williams
  b. James Derham
  c. Charles R. Drew
  d. Rebecca Cole

11 Benjamin Banneker, Black inventor and scientist was born November 19, 1731 in
  a. Ellicott, Maryland
  b. Jackson, Mississippi
  c. Austin, Texas
  d. Ottumwa, Iowa

12 Who composed "Carry Me Back To Old Virginny"?
  a. Duke Ellington
  b. Count Basie
  c. James A. Bland
  d. Alice Walker

NICKNAMES; SPORTS

You probaby know these people by their nicknames listed here, but these aren't their real names. See how many you can get correct. Write the number preceding their nickname alongside their real name.

NICK NAME		**REAL NAME**
1 Dr. J	____	Marvin Barnes
2 Louisville Lip	____	William Perry
3 Bad News	____	Jesse Owens
4 Mongoose	____	Marvin Hagler
5 Refrigerator	____	Ed Jones
6 Ebony Express	____	Archie Moore
7 Marvelous	____	Julius Erving
8 Too Tall	____	Joe Louis
9 Brown Bomber	____	Muhammad Ali
10 Smokin Joe	____	Willie Mays
11 Say-Hey-Kid	____	Olajuwon & Sampson
12 Twin Towers	____	Joe Frazier
13 The Dream	____	Walter Payton
14 Magic	____	Akeem Olajuwon
15 Sweetness	____	Earvin Johnson

RHYTHM AND BLUES;
WHO SANG THAT SONG #2

Here are 15 top Rhythm and Blues hits from 1972-73 by Black singers. Identify the singer that sang each song. Write the number preceding the song alongside the singer.

	SONG		SINGER
1	"Get On The Good Foot"	_____	Staple Singers
2	"We're Almost Home"	_____	Solomon Burke
3	"Are You Man Enough"	_____	Ike & Tina Turner
4	"Little Ghetto Boy"	_____	Michael Jackson
5	"Sweet Sixteen"	_____	James Brown
6	"Slippin Into Darkness"	_____	Stevie Wonder
7	"I'll Take You There"	_____	War
8	"I Gotcha"	_____	Four Tops
9	"Nut Bush City Limits"	_____	Jerry Butler
10	"Lean On Me"	_____	Joe Tex
11	"Slippin Into Darkness"	_____	B.B. King
12	"Rockin Robin"	_____	War
13	"I Only Have Eyes For You"	_____	Ramsey Lewis
14	"Living For The City"	_____	Bill Withers
15	"The World Is A Ghetto"	_____	Donny Hathaway

INVENTIONS BY BLACKS; 1834-1950

Black Americans contributed greatly to the invention of many items. Some of the earlier inventions by Black Americans were concealed and unrecorded, this was partially due to Black people being slaves and the refusal of some Black people to patent their inventions. The following questions are about inventions by Black Americans.

1. Who invented the Corn Husking Machine, patent August 14, 1883?

2. Who was the inventor of the Steam Boiler Furnace June 3, 1884, Patent No. 299,894?

3. Who invented the Railway Telegraphy, November 15 1887?

4. Who invented the Toggie Harpoon, 1848?

5. Who was the inventor of the Corn Planter, patent October 14, 1834?

6. Who invented the Thermostat and Temperature Control System, February 23, 1960?

7. Who invented the Air Conditioning Unit, patent July 12, 1949?

8. Who invented the Lasting Machine, patent September 22, 1891?

9. Who invented a method for making Carbon Filaments for the Maxim Electric Incandescent Lamp?

10 Who invented the Sugar Refiner (Evaporating Pan) patent December 10, 1846?

11 Who invented the Galvanic Battery, patent August 14, 1888?

12 Who invented the Curtain Rod, patent August 30, 1892?

13 Who invented the Lawn Sprinkler, patent May 4, 1897?

14 Who invented the Rotary Engine, patent July 5, 1892?

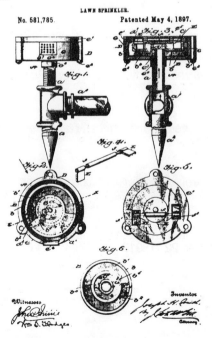

15 Patent March 17, 1896, the Street Sweeper was invented by who?

16 Patent April 26, 1862, the Ironing Board was invented by who?

17 Patent August 23, 1892, the Horse Shoe was invented by who?

18 Who invented the Cotton Planter, patent August 31, 1836?

19 Who invented the Ice Cream Mold patent February 2, 1892?

20 Who invented the Golf-Tee, patent December 12, 1899?

21 Who invented the Gas Burner, patent April 4, 1899?

22 Who invented the Ticket Dispensing Machine, patent June 27, 1937?

23 Who invented the Two-Cycle Gasoline Engine, patent November 28, 1950?

24 Who invented the Automatic Gear Shift, December 6, 1932, patent No. 1,889,814?

25 Who invented the Wagon, October 18, 1870, patent No. 108,419?

26 Patent May 7, 1878, the Fire Escape Ladder was invented by who?

27 Who invented the Mop, patent June 13, 1893?

28 Who invented the Potato Digger, patent January 21, 1891?

29 Who invented the Starter Generator, patent July 12, 1949?

30 Patent July 18, 1899 the Folding Bed was invented by who?

31 Who invented the Pencil Sharpener, patent November 23, 1897?

32 Who invented the Elevator, patent No. 371,207 October 11, 1887?

33 Who invented Caps for bottles, patent September 13, 1898?

34 September 1881 patent No. 247,097 the Electric Lamp. Who invented it?

35 Who invented the Ironing Table, patent May 12, 1874?

36 Who invented the Steam Dome, patent June 1885?

37 The Steam Gage, patent August 25, 1896 was invented by who?

38 Who was the inventor of the Fountain Pen, patent January 7, 1890?

39 Patent February 5, 1884, the Egg Beater was invented by who?

40 Who invented the Plasterers' Hawk, patent July 9, 1895 patent No. 542,419.

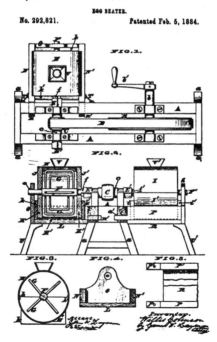

41 Who invented the Riding Saddle, patent October 6, 1896?

42 Who invented the Ladder Scaffold Support, patent August 5, 1879?

43 Who invented Spring Seat for chairs, patent April 3, 1888?

44 Patent January 10, 1888 the Railway Signal was invented by who?

45 Who invented the Bicycle Frame, patent October 10, 1899?

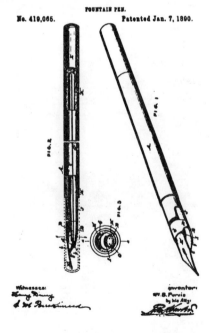

61

46 He invented the Lunar Surface Ultra Violet Camera Spectrograph in 1972.

47 Who invented the Lock, patent July 23, 1889 patent No. 407,738.

48 Patent May 23, 1871, the Locomotive Smoke Stack was invented by who?

49 Who invented the Lawn Mower, patent May 9, 1899 ?

50 Who invented the Luggage Carrier, patent October 10, 1899?

BLACK WRITERS

1. His books include: "Before the Mayflower" (1962) "The Negro Mood" and other essays (1964) "What Manner of Man" (a biography of Martin Luther King published in 1964) "The Shaping of Black America" (1974). Who is he?

2. Poet, Novelist, Anthologist; 1902-1973, was one of the most productive Black writers of the 20th Century. His books for young people include; "We Have Tomorrow" (1945) and "Story of The Negro" (1948). Who was he?

3. Dramatist, Essayist, Poet, a writer of drama and one of the founders of the Black Arts/West in the Filmore District of San Francisco. He presents his material in a realistic and naturalistic style. In production from 1965 to 1968 he wrote; "The Rally, How Do You Do" "Goin' a Buffalo", "In The Wine Time". Who was he?

4. In 1942 she published "For My People" and two years later, was awarded a Rosenwald Fellowship for creative writing. Her other works are; "How I Wrote Jubilee" "October Journey", "Prophets For A New Day". Who is she?

5. 1859-1932, Novelist, was the first Black writer to deal with the race question from the Negro's point of view. His first novel "The House Behind The Cedars" (1900) dealt with a young girl's attempt to pass for White. His final novel "The Colonel's Dream" was published in 1905. Who was he?

6 1872-1906, Poet, the first Black poet to gain a national reputation in the United States, was also the first to use Negro dialect within the formal structure of his work. His first book of poetry "Oak and Ivy" was privately printed in 1893. Some of his later works included "Lyrics Of Love and Laughter" (1903), "Lyrics of Sunshine and Shadow" (1905). Who was he?

7 Poet, born in Knoxville, Tennessee 1943, she studied at Fisk University and at the University of Pennsylvania. Her first book of poetry, "Black Feeling, Black Talk" (mid-1960), was followed by "Black Judgment" in 1968. Who is she?

8 Novelist, born in Washington, D.C. in 1941, and educated at the University of Pennsylvania and at Oxford University where he was a Rhodes Scholar. In 1974, he was a professor of English at the University of Wyoming. His first novel, "A Glance Away" was published in 1967 when he was 26 years old. His second novel, "Hurry Home" was published in 1970. Who is he?

9 Novelist, born in Jefferson City, Missouri, educated at Ohio State University, has lived in France and now lives in Spain. In 1945, he completed his first novel "If He Hollers, Let Him Go", his second book, "The Lonely Crusade" (1947), "Cotton Comes To Harlem" (1965). Who is he?

BLACK MAYORS; PAST AND PRESENT

1. November 1974, he became the first Black person to be elected Mayor of Washington, D.C. since the Reconstruction Era. Who is he?

2. November 1977, he was elected Mayor of New Orleans.

3. October 1979, Richard Arrington became the first Black Mayor of what city?

4. April 29, 1983 Harold Washington was sworn in as the first Black Mayor of what city?

5. He was elected the first Black Mayor of Philadelphia November, 1983.

6. October 1981, this former U.N. Ambassador was elected Mayor of Atlanta.

7. March 1977, Henry L. Marsh III is elected Mayor of what city?

8. May 1973, he was elected Mayor of Los Angles.

9. He was elected Mayor of Detroit in November, 1973.

10. October 1973, Maynard Jackson was elected Mayor of what city?

11. In 1972, Johnny Ford became the first Black person to take the Mayor's oath in what city?

12 September 1972, he became the first Black person to be elected Mayor of Pritchard, Alabama.

13 June 1970, he became the first Black Mayor of Newark, New Jersey.

14 November 1967, Richard G. Hatcher became the first Black Mayor of what city?

15 He was sworn in on November 13, 1967 and became the first Black person to serve as Mayor of a major American city. Who was he and for what city?

BLACK COWBOYS

1 Known as Cherokee Bill, a notorious Black outlaw, born in Ft. Concho, Texas 1876. Cherokee Bill was once caught and taken to Ft. Smith, Arkansas for trial he was sentenced to hang but escaped. He was caught again and hanged on March 17, 1896.
What was his real name?

2 Nicknamed "80 John", because the ranch which he worked on used the branding iron "80". He made his first cattle drive at age fifteen. In 1885 when he was twenty-five, he purchased almost 160 acres of land and some cattle. At the time of his death in 1939, he left an estate totaling 1,200 acres and 600 head of cattle free of debt.

3 Billed as "The Dusky Demon", he was born in 1870, near Austin, Texas. He was the originator of steer wrestling and called the man who invented bulldogging He traveled throughout the United States, England and South America with Will Rogers, Tom Mix and other cowboys. He died at the age of 71, trying to tame and rope a wild horse. In 1971 he was enshrined in the National Rodeo Hall of Frame.
What was his real name?

4 Isom Dart, a Black outlaw born a slave in Arkansas. After the Civil War, he went to Mexico and joined a gang of horse thieves. Later he moved to Brown's Hole, Colorado, fell in love with an Indian woman named Tickup. When she left him for another man, he joined the Tip Gault Gang. Eventually the gang, except for Isom were killed in a fight. He moved to Oklahoma, where he tried to lead a quiet life raising cotton. Later Dart went back to Brown's Hole and tried to lead a fair law-abiding life. In 1900, he was killed by Tom Horn a range detective.
What was Dart's real name?

Isom Dart

Denver Public Library, Western History Department

68

Bill Pickett

Denver Public Library, Western History Department

Nat Love

Denver Public Library, Western History Department

5 Born a slave in Tennessee in 1854, known as "Deadwood Dick", he was the most famous Black cowboy in history. After the Civil War, he went West where he earned a living by breaking in wild horses. What was his real name?

HISTORIC LANDMARKS
OF BLACK AMERICANS

No more substantial testimony to the Black role in the growth and development of America can be found than the numerous historical landmarks in various regions of the Country which are associated with Black Americans.
How many can you identify?

1. This chapel on Alcorn Campus was built in 1838. It's the oldest building on Alcorn University's Campus. The chapel symbolizes the importance of Alcorn as the first Black land grant college in the United States. On May 11, 1976 the chapel was designated a National Historic Landmark by the Department Of Interior.
What is the name and location of the chapel?

2. Site of a Fort at which Black soldiers stayed during the Indian Wars. Two of the soldiers, Benjamin Brown and Isaiah Mays received Congressional Medals Of Honor while on duty at this fort.
What is the name and location of the Fort?

3. Unveiled in 1974 is the first monument to a Black person. The $400,000 mounment is erected on public land in the nation's capitol. It is located in Lincoln Park. It is inscribed with these words: " I leave you love, I leave you hope, I leave you the challenge of developing confidence in one another. I leave you a thirst for education. I leave you respect for the use of power. I leave you faith. I leave you racial dignity." In 1904 she established the Daytona Normal and Industrial Institute for Black girls. In 1926 she merged with Cookman Institute of Jacksonvile. She helped President Roosevelt organize the national "You" Administration. In 1936 she became Director of the Division of Black Affairs.
What is the name and location of the monument?

4 She was the first Black newspaper woman in America and lived in this house from 1881-1886. She was also a educator, lawyer, writer and antislavery abolitionist. During the Civil War, she held the position of recruiting officer for the Union Army to enlist Black volunteers. On December 8, 1976 the house she lived in from 1881-1886 was designated a National Historic Landmark.
What is the name and location of the house?

5 This was the boyhood home of this late nineteenth and early twentieth century Black expatriate painter whose work earned him recognition in the United States and Europe. He was the first Black to be elected to the National Academy of Design. On May 11, 1976 the homesite was designated a Historical Landmark by the Department of Interior.
What is the name and location of the homesite?*

6 This was the site of the only Revolutionary War battle, that an all Black unit, the 1st. Rhode Island Regiment participated in. The unit joined John Sullivan's army in attacking British Garrison troops on Newport. On May 30, 1974 the site was named a National Historic Landmark.
What is the name of the site?

7 He was born Haiti to a French Mariner father and Black mother, immigrated to French Louisiana and became a fur trapper. He established trading posts on the sites of the present cities of Michigan City, Indiana; Peoria ,Illinois and Huron, Michigan. Of all the trading posts, the most important post was on the site of Chicago, Illinois. This was the site he constructed a log home for his wife and family. It is recognized as the first settlement of Chicago. On May 11, 1976 the homesite was designated a National Historic Landmark.
What is the name and location of this home site?

8 This was the home of the baseball player who in 1949 became the first Black to play in the major leagues. His signing to a baseball contract broke the color barrier to Black participation in professional sports. While playing for the Brooklyn Dodger, he lived for many years in the Borough of New York City, where he played baseball. On may 11, 1976, the residence was designated a National Historic Landmark.
What is the name of the residence?

9 From 1941 to 1946 this was the residence of a Black poet and writer who was often called the father of the Harlem Renaissance. He was born in Jamaica, British West Indies. On December 8, 1976 his residence was named a National Historic Landmark by the Department fo Interior.
What is the name of the residence?

10 In 1903 this Black woman founded the successful Saint Luke Penny Savings Bank, to become the first woman to establish and head a bank. Her life and career have inspired many. In addition to being the first woman president of a bank, she was editor of a newspaper which was considered to be one of the best journals in America. The house she lived in is located in the Jackson Ward Historic District of Richmond. On May 15, 1975, it was declared a National Historic Landmark.
What was the name of the house?

11 From 1920 to 1939 this was the home address of a noted Black physican and teacher, best remembered for his pioneer work in discovering ways to preserve blood plasma. On May 11, 1976 this house was named a National Historic Landmark by the Department of Interior.
What is the name of the house?

12 Dr. King was laid to rest in this cemetery. A marble crypt was inscribed with the words he used to conclude his famous speech delivered at the 1968 March on Washington. The words, taken from an old slave song are; "Free at last free at last, Thank God Almighty I'm free at last." This cemetery was founded in 1886 by Blacks.
What is the name and location of the cemetery?

13 This institute is a world-famous center for agricultural research and extension work. Opened on July 4, 1881 with $2,000 appropriation from the Alabama State Legislature. It consited of 30 students and one teacher, Booker T. Washington. In 1882, Washington moved the school to a 100 acre plantation. Next to Washington, the most famous person to be associated with the institute was George Washington Carver, who became Director of Agricultural research in 1896. Today the institute covers nearly 5,000 acres and has over 150 buildings. Notable places to visit there are the George Washington Carver Museum and Booker T. Washington Monument. The institute is also the home of the George Washington Carver Foundation, a research center founded by George Washington Carver in 1940.
What is the name and location of the institute?

14 Founded in 1867, this University is the largest institution of higher learning established for Blacks in the Post-Civil War period. Covering more than 50 acres, the campus grounds and physical plant are valued at more than 40 million dollars. Of particular interest is the Founders Library, which contains more than 300,000 volumes and includes the Moorland Collection, which is one of the finest collections on Black life and history in the United States.
What is the name and location of the University?

Jim Beckwourth

Denver Public Library, Western History Department

15 Educator and founder of Tuskegee Institute, he is the only Black American honored by a plaque in the Hall Of Fame, in New York University.
What is the name and location of the plaque?

16 A Senator from Mississippi he was the first Black American to serve a full term in the U. S. Senate from 1875 to 1881. He was born in Farmville, Virginia. In 1861 prior to the Civil War, he escaped to Hannibal, Missouri and set up a school for Blacks. He studied at Oberlin College in Oberlin, Ohio. He moved to Mississippi and became a wealthy planter. His positions in Mississippi included that of tax collector, sheriff, superintendent of schools, for the county and a member of the levee board in Mississippi. He was elected by the Mississippi State Legislature to the U.S. Senate in 1874. On May 15,1975 his house was designated a National Historic Landmark.,
What is the name and location of the house?

17 This was the first training school for Black nurses in the United States. It was founded By Dr. Daniel Hale Williams, the renowned surgeon who in 1893 performed the first successful operation on the human heart.
What is the name and location of the school?

18 One of the leading institutions in the South for the training of Black teachers, this college was founded in 1904 on "faith an a dollar-and-a-half." The founder was a advisor to Presidents Franklin D. Roosevelt and Harry S. Truman. She was one of the most powerful and influential Blacks in the United States.
What is the name and location of the college?

19 The home of this distinguished Afro-American diplomat and scholar who served as Under Secretary of the United Nations and in 1949 received the Noble Peace Prize for his contributions to peace in the Middle East. This house was designated a National Historic Landmark on May 11, 1976 by the Department of Interior.
What is the name and location of the house?

20 James Beckwourth, the first Black frontiersman for who Beckwourth Pass was named is located where?

Denver Public Library, Western History Department

U.S. Army, 25th Infantry Company B, Fort Snelling 1883-1888

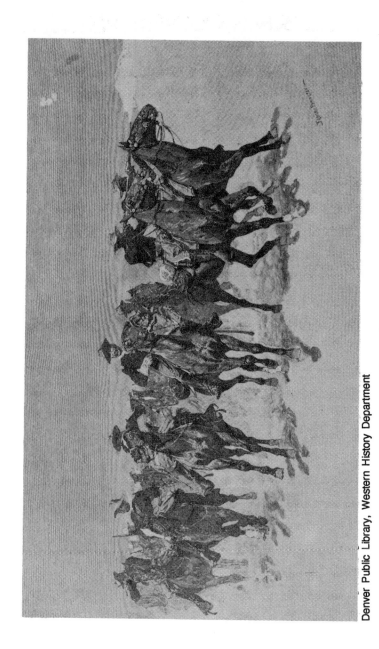

Denver Public Library, Western History Department

U.S. Armed Forces, Army Cavalry

BLACK QUOTATIONS

1. "No person is your friend who demands your silence, or denies your right to grow", was said by who?
   - a. Alice Walker
   - b. Billie Holiday
   - c. Phillis Wheatly
   - d. Shirley Chisholm

2. "Say it loud, I'm Black and I'M proud", was said by who?
   - a. Booker T. Washington
   - b. James Brown
   - c. Malcolm X
   - d. Marcus Garvey

3. "No two people on earth are alike, and it's got to be that way in music or it isn't music", was said by who?
   - a. Billie Holiday
   - b. Phillis Wheatly
   - c. Ray Charles
   - d. James Brown

4. "Education is our passport to the future, for tomorrow belongs to the people who prepare for it today", was said by who?
   - a. Booker T. Washington
   - b. W.E.B. Dubois
   - c. Malcolm X
   - d. James Baldwin

5. "If a man is called to be a streetsweeper, he should sweep streets even as Michelangelo painted, or Beethoven composed music or Shakespeare wrote poetry. He should sweep streets so well that all the hosts of heaven and earth will pause to say, here lived a great streetsweeper who did his job well", was said by who?
   - a. Martin L. King Jr
   - b. Frederick Douglass
   - c. Marcus Garvey
   - d. George W. Carver

6. "A Race without authority and power is a Race without respect", was said by who?
   - a. James Baldwin
   - b. St. Clair Drake
   - c. Marcus Garvey
   - d. Nat Turner

7 "I have a dream that my four little children will one day live in a Nation where they will not be judged by the color of their skin, but by the content of their character", was said by who?
    a. Frederick Douglass   c. Martin L. King Jr.
    b. Booker T. Washington   d. none of these

8 "Every Race and every Nation should be judged by the best it has been able to produce, not by the worst", was said by who?
    a. James W. Johnson   c. Julian Bond
    b. W.E.B. DuBois   d. Harriet Tubman

9 "Men may not get all they pay for in this World, but they must certainly pay for all they get", was said by who?
    a. Sojourner Truth   c. James Baldwin
    b. Malcolm X   d. Frederick Douglass

10 "We may have all come over in different ships, but we're in the same boat now", was said by who?
    a. Whitney Young   c. Nat Turner
    b. Marcus Garvey   d. none of these

11 "Injustice anywhere is a threat to justice everywhere", was said by who?
    a. W.E.B. DuBois   c. Frederick Douglass
    b. Martin L. King   d. James Baldwin

12 "No Race can prosper till it learns that there is as much dignity in tilling a field as in writing a poem", was said by who?
    a. David Walker   c. James Baldwin
    b. Booker T. Washington   d. Nat Turner

13 "There was one of two things I had a right to, Liberty, or death; if I could not have one, I would have the other; for no man should take me alive; I should fight for my Liberty as long as my strength lasted, and when the time came for me to go the Lord would let them take me", was said by who?
    a. Harriet Tubman   c. Shirley Chisholm
    b. Billie Holiday   d. Alice Walker

14 "There is a debt to the Negro people which America can never repay. At least then, They must make amends", was said by who?
    a. Hiram R. Revels   c. Sojourner Truth
    b. Joseph H. Rainey   d. Harriet Tubman

15 "If there is no struggle, there is no progress", was said by who?
    a. Marcus Garvey   c. W.E.B. DuBois
    b. Frederick Douglass   d. Alice Walker

BLACK WOMEN

1 The first Black woman State Legislator, she was the youngest of nine children, born in Princess Anne, Maryland, June 27, 1893. In 1918, she traveled the country as field secrataty for the YWCA, developing programs for Black working girls and students. On November 8, 1938 she became the first Black women in history to be given a seat in the United States House of Representatives. She founded the United Nations Council of Philadelphia in 1945 which later became the World Affairs Council. March 28, 1965 she died in her sleep. Name this great woman.

2 In 1922 she received her air pilot's license from the Federation Aeronautique Internationale in France, to become the first Black woman pilot. Born January 26, 1893, Atlanta, Texas she was the 12th of 13 children. On April 30, 1926, she was asked to give an exhibition for the Jacksonville, FL Negro Welfare League. Flying at 110 mph at an altitude of 3500 feet, she put her plane into a 1500 foot nose dive and never came out. Who was she?

3 The first Black woman in the United States to establish a school that became a four year accredited college. She was born in Mayesville, South Carolina in 1875. Primarily an educator she became invovled in government affairs. In 1930 President Herbert Hoover appointed her to the White House Conference on Child Health. Several years later. President Franklin D. Roosevelt appointed her Director of Negro Affairs in the National Youth Administration and his special advisor on Minority Affairs. In 1945 she was special emissary of the State Department of the United Nations Conference. 1952 she was the personal representative of President Harry S. Truman at Liberia's inauguration ceremonies. She died May 18, 1955. Who was this great woman?

4 Born in Clarksville, Tennessee in 1867 she became the first Black woman in America to earn a Doctor of Dental surgery degree. She attended Gaines Public High School in Cincinnati. Graduated from high school in 1887. Entered the University of Michigan Dental School where she received her DDS Degree in 1890. Married James S. Nelson in 1895. Who was she?

5 Chosen unanimously by the Progressive Party Convention in 1952, she became the first Black women to run for the nation's second highest political office, Vice President of the United States. Born 1890 in Little Compton, R.I. she studied at UCLA, Brown University and Columbia University. While a resident of Los Angeles, she was the editor and publisher of the California Eagle, the oldest Black newspaper on the West Coast. She died in 1961. Who was she?

6 Because of her innovations in the cosmetics business she became one of the wealthiest and most famous women of her race. Born to exslave parents in Delta, LA, Sarah McWilliams was orphaned at the age of seven married at 14 and left a widow with a small child at the age of 20. In 1910 she went to Indianapolis to begin the manufacture of her hair preparations, later adding a complete line of toiletries and cosmetics to her products. As her business expanded, she established many beauty schools across the country. In the process she became the first Black women millionaire. She made large bequests to the NAACP, Tuskegee Institute and Bethune Cookman College and stipulated in her will that two-thirds of the profits of her company should be given to charitable organizations. Who was she?

7 A physician who received her medical degree with honors from Tufts Medical School in Massachusetts, she began her medical career in Washington D.C. She served for several years on the Board of Directors of the Southeast Settlement House. She succeeded Mary McLeod Bethune as President of The National Council of Negro Women. In 1951 she was sent by the United States Labor Department to study health problems of women in Germany. She later visted Africa as a delegate to an international conference of women of African descent. Besides maintaining her own medical practice, she is a full professor of preventive medicine at the Howard School of Medicine. What is her name?

8 She was the first Black newspaper woman in the North American Continent. She published Canada's first anti-slavery newspaper, "The Provincial Freeman." in 1856 she married. When President Lincoln called for men to fight in the Union Army, she returned to the United States. On August 15, 1863 she was appointed Army recruiting officer to enlist Black volunteers in the state of Indiana. After the war, she moved to Washington D.C. where she enrolled in Howard University Law Department. She became the second Black woman in the United States to earn A law degree in 1883. She died in 1893. Who was she?

RHYTHM AND BLUES;
WHO SANG THAT SONG

1. In 1967, this Soul superstar demanded "Respect" and she got it. She reached #1 on the charts with her hit song. Who is she?
   a. Tina Turner
   b. Roberta Flack
   c. Aretha Franklin
   d. none of these

2. Michael Jackson set a record in 1984, by winning how many Grammy Awards?
   a. 1
   b. 4
   c. 3
   d. 8

3. Anthony Gourdine and his group had a smash hit in 1958 called "Tears On My Pillow". Who was Anthony's backup singers?
   a. The Imperials
   b. Raydio
   c. Flames
   d. none of these

4. Before setting out on a solo career, this performer was the lead singer for Harold Melvin and The Blue Notes. Who is he?
   a. Wilson Pickett
   b. Jackie Wilson
   c. Teddy Pendergrass
   d. Sam Cooke

5. What Motown Group made "Dancing In The street" popular in 1964?
   a. Martha & The Vandellas
   b. Temptations
   c. Marvelettes
   d. Supremes

6. Who was the Detroit singer with the big voice who sang "Lonely Teardrops"?
   a. David Ruffin
   b. James Brown
   c. Otis Redding
   d. Jackie Wilson

7. Lionel Richies's first #1 solo hit was
   a. "Truly"
   b. "Sail On"
   c. "You and Me"
   d. "All Night Long"

8 They first hit the charts as an R & B Group in 1961, and had a disco hit in 1980 with "Working My Way Back To You" and "Cupid". Name them
    a. The Miracles   c. The Temptations
    b. The Spinners   d. The Four Tops

9 In his 1961 hit, Lee Dorsey was "Sittin' Here La La Waitin' for my
    a. ya ya   c. ma ma
    b. ta ta   d. da da

10 Who was the first to hit the chart with "I Heard It Through The Grapevine"?
    a. Gladys Knight & Pips   c. Marvin Gaye
    b. Martha & The Vandellas   d. Supremes

11 Henry Saint Clair Fredericks composed the score for "Sounder" and has been releasing rhythmic albums since 1967. We know him as
    a. Taj Mahal   c. Bo Diddley
    b. Isaac Hayes   d. none of these

12 This lead singer, on the Drifters' smash hit "Save The Last Dance For Me" went on to have solo hits of his own, including the smash hit "Stand By Me". Name him
    a. Ben E. King   c. Chuck Berry
    b. Isaac Hayes   d. Fats Domino

13 Who was Marvin Gaye's singing partner on the 1967 hit "Your Precious Love"?
    a. Aretha Franklin   c. Roberta Flack
    b. Tammi Terrel   d. Dionne Warwick

14 "Pops", Cleo, Mavis and Yvonne comprised what popular musical family?
   a. Sly & The Family Stone   c. Soul Children
   b. The Exciters   d. The Staple Singers

15 In 1981 the Pointer Sisters were looking for "A Man With
   a. A Slow Hand"   c. Another Man"
   b. A Drink"   d. A Car"

SOME WHO MADE A DIFFERENCE

1. George Washington Carver was born a slave where?

2. Alice Walker, poet, novelist, was educated at what college in Atlanta, Georgia?

3. His epitaph reads, "He could have added fortune to fame, but caring for neither, he found happiness and honor in being helpful to the World".

4. What is Booker T. Washington's middle name?

5. George Washington Carver is buried alongside who?

6. "I nebber run my train off de track, and I nebber lost a passenger" was once said by who?

7. He became the first Black to win the prestigous Nobel Peace Prize.

8. She was the first Black to sing with the Metropolitan Opera Company.

9. He was the first Black admitted to the University of Mississippi.

10. She was the first Black student to graduate from the University of Alabama.

11. January 18, 1966, he was sworn in as Secretary of Housing and Urban Development and became the first Black Cabinet member.

12 He was named coach of the Boston Celtics basketball team and became the first Black to coach an established team in professional athletics. Who was he?

13 He was the first Black elected Mayor of Pritchard, Alabama.

14 Martin Luther King, Jr. was assassinated when—month, date and year?

15 Ray Charles was how old when he lost his sight?
16

16 He went by such names as: Delta John, Johnny Lee, Texas Slim, Boogle Man, Birmingham Sam.

17 He became well known as the "Father of the Blues".

18 Benjamin Banneker, Black inventor and scientist, was born November 9, 1731 where?

19 This Agricultural Scientist never patented any of the many discoveries he made while at Tuskegee.

20 True or False: Charles Drew was appointed director of the American Red Cross blood donor project.

21 True or False: Lewis Howard Latimer was employed by Alexander Graham Bell, to make the patent drawings for the first telephone.

22 ANAID is the name of what Black female superstar's production company?

23 Satchel Paige was born September, 1904 in what city and state?

24 True or False: Cab Calloway was born on Christmas Day, 1907 in Rochester, New york.

25 Who wrote "There is no defense or security for any of us except in the highest intelligence and development of all"?

26 "A Race without authority and power is a Race without respect", was said by who?

27 "We may have all come over in different ships, but we're in the same boat now", was said by who?

28 1745-1796 he was born in St. Marc Haiti, the son of a successful French man who migrated to Haiti from Marseilies, France. Who was he?

29 How many times did Roy Campanella win the Most Valuable Player's Award?

30 True or False: In 1916 Fritz Pollard was the first Black person to play in the Rose Bowl.

31 True or False: In 1890 George Dixon of Halifax Nova Scotia became the first Black person to win a World Boxing Title.

32 in 1960 he became the first boxer in history to regain the heavyweight title.

33 His boxing record of a 145 career knockouts may never be broken.

34 True or False: The Harlem Globetrotters were established in 1927.

35 Who won the Oscar for the best actor in "Lilies of The Field"?

36 True or False: In 1955, Nat King Cole starred in his own T.V. Show.

37 Who created the characters on the Fat Albert Cartoon Show?

38 In 1940 Hattie McDaniel won an Oscar for Best Supporting Actress for her performance in what?

39 Who's entertainment career began as "Silent Sam, The Dancing Midget"?

40 Who founded the Association For The Study of Negro Life and History?

41 True or False: Peter Salem, Salem Poor and others are among Black Americans to fight heroically at Bunker Hill, 1775.

42 True or false: Ray Charles plays Clarinet, Organ, Piano, Saxophone, and Trumpet.

43 October 27, 1954 he became the first Black General in the United States Air Force. Name him.

44 January 18, 1949, he was elected Chairman of House Expenditures Committee. He became the first Black person to head a standing committee of Congress. Who is he?

45 August 1954, he was named Under Secretary of the United Nations.

46 Novemberr 10, 1960 he was named Associate Press Secretary to President elect Kennedy.

47 Who declared: "I Have Been to The Mountain Top"?

48 Who declared: "I Have a Dream"?

49 He was the first Black person to take the Governor's oath in the Virgin Islands.

50 He made history by being the first Black person named to the Federal Reserve Board.

51 She received the Motion Picture Academy's highest award in 1940 as the year's best supporting actress in "Gone With The Wind", to become the first Black person ever to win an Oscar. Born on June 10, 1898 in Wichita, Kansas moved to Denver, Colorado as a child. In addition to her movie roles, she also had great success on radio during the 1930's. Who was she?

52 1606-1670, famous pupil of the Spanish painter Velasquez, he was born in Seville, spain. Who was he?

53 This famous Black scientist discovered an ingredient to relieve inflammatory arthritis from soy beans. Name him.

54 He could "float like a butterfly and sting like a bee". Name him.

55 True or False: Arthur Ashe quit compatitive tennis because of a heart attack.

56 True or False: Booker Taliaferro Washington was born a slave in Franklin County, Virginia in 1863.

57 Name the first Black person to play major league baseball in 1884 for the Toledo Mudhens.

58 His aptitude in mathematics and knowledge of Astronomy enabled him to predict the Solar Eclipse of 1789. Who was he?

59 The only fighter ever to hold three titles at the same time was who?

60 President of the National Urban League, he was awarded the U.S. Medal of Freedom. Name him.

61 True or False: The first Black heavyweight boxing champion was Jack Johnson.

62 True or False: WERD, the first Black-owned radio station, opened in Atlanta, October, 1949.

63 She became the first Black person to win the Pulitzer Prize for her book of Poetry, "Annie Allen".

64 In April, 1984 the University of Georgetown, basketball team won the NCAA Championship and this Black coach became the first to lead a team to a Division I NCAA National Title. Who is he?

65 July, 1955, he was appointed administrative aide to President Eisenhower and became the first Black person to hold an executive position on the White House staff.

66 Who was the first Black woman to be honored on a postage stamp?

67 Jamaica 1911, he forms the Universal Negro Improvement Association.

68 1863,- Union Black Troops are organized into 165 regiments of light and heavy artillery, cavalry, infantry and engineers. They were called what?

69 Who was the first Black person to win a Best Actor Emmy?

70 April 8, 1974 Hank Aaron broke Babe Ruth's major league baseball record by hitting his 715th home run in what stadium?

71 In 1950, he became the first Black person to play organized hockey. He played for the Atlantic City Seagulls. Name him.

72 January 16, 1978 NASA named three Black astronauts, to the space program. Name them.

73 In Central City, Colorado, there is a chair in the Opera House which is dedicated to a Black woman who lived there from 1859 until her death in 1877 at age eighty-five. Who was she?

74 In 1904, she established the Daytona Normal and Industrial Institute for Black girls. In 1926, she merged with Cookman Institute to form the Bethune and Cookman College. She helped President Roosevelt organize the National Youth Administration. In 1935 she received the Spingarn Award. Who was she?

75 She is believed to have led some 300 slaves to freedom via the Underground Railroad. Born a slave in Maryland, Mississippi, she fled at the age of 25, only to return South at least 19 times to lead others to freedom. She never lost one of her passengers in transit. During the Civil War, she served as a spy for Union forces. Who was she?

WHO SANG THAT SONG "SIXTIES"

1. "Only You," "The Great Pretender" and "My Prayer," were sang by who?

2. "Blueberry Hill," was this singers' highest charted song.
   Name him.

3. In 1967 "Little Old Man" was a hit song for who?

4. "Playboy," "Don't Mess With Bill" and "Please Mr. Postman" were sang by who?

5. Who sang "Shotgun," "What Does It Take" and "These Eyes?"

6. Who sang "Busted," "What'd I Say" and "Cryin Time?"

7. Who sang "Dance To The Music," "Everybody Is A Star" and "Everyday People?"

8. Who sang "Cupid," "Chain Gang" and "You Send Me?"

9. Who sang "Uptown," "Then He Kissed Me" and "Da Doo Run Run?"

10. The "Twist", "Finger Poppin Time" and "Let's Go, Let's Go" were sang by who?

THE BLACK SCREEN

1 1974, Sidney Poitier stars and directs this light-hearted comedy, with such talents as Bill Cosby and Harry Belafonte.
Name the movie.

2 1974, Moms Mabley and Slappy White make rare film appearances in this goodnatured comedy.
Name the movie.

3 Diana Ross and Billy Dee Williams star in this 1975 romantic drama about a woman who fulfills her dream to become a celebrity fashion model.
Name the movie.

4 In this 1965 movie, Nat Cole is featured as a traveling minstrel.
Name the movie.

5 This 1966 movie was produced by Sammy Davis, Jr, along with Cicely Tyson, Louis Armstrong and Ossie Davis, in the story of a problem-ridden musician.
Name the movie.

6 This 1969 controversial drama takes a close look at slavery as it occured in the United States. It stars Ossie Davis along with Dionne Warwick.
Name the movie.

7 This 1969 version of the Liam O'Flaherty story, stars Julian Mayfield, Ruby Dee, Raymond St. Jacques, Frank Silvera, and Roscoe Lee Browne. Booker T. Jones composed the music.
Name the movie.

8 This 1969 documentary on the late Martin Luther King Jr.s' "Poor People's March," shows Dr. King conferring with aides, speaking at rallies and traveling as he solicits support for, and develops the details of the March.
Name the documentary.

9 James Earl Jones stars in this 1972 film version of the best-selling novel about the first Black man to be elected president of the United States.
Name the movie.

10 In 1978 Bill Cosby and Richard Pryor star in this Neil Simon comedy about guests at a California hotel.
Name the movie.

11 Richard Pryor and Pam Grier star in this drama based on the life of Wendell Scott, one of the countries most prominent Black race car drivers.
Name the movie.

12 In 1976 Bill Cosby stars in this Twentieth Century Fox, comedy about the operation of an ambulance service.
Name the movie.

13 1978, Billy Dee Williams stars in the title role of this biographical drama about a noted ragtime composer.
Name the movie.

14 Billy Dee Williams, Richard Pryor and James Earl Jones, star in this humorous drama about the early Black baseball teams that barnstormed around the country.
Name the movie.

15 Richard Roundtree made his film debut with director Gordon Parks in this adventure story about a Black New York City private eye.
Name the movie.

16 Marki Bey stars as a young nightclub owner on a Caribbean island. When her boyfriend is slain, she seeks out the forces of voodoo to avenge his death. A rare Black horror film.
Name the film.

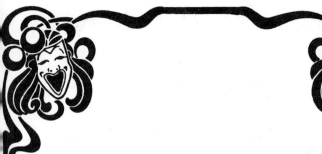

17 Pearl Bailey and Red Foxx star in this comedy about a married couple whose son presents them with an unusual problem.
Name the movie.

18 This Reggae singer stars in this Jamaican-produced film, about the singer and his encounters with the system. The film was a first from the islands and a revealing portrait of Caribbean life.
Name the singer.

19 In 1973 Raymond St. Jacques makes his directing and producing debut in this film, based on the life of Southern society, with emphasis on numbers running.
Name the movie.

20 In 1977 Richard Pryor starred in three different roles in this comedy-drama, about compromise and sticking with one's convictions.
Name the movie.

BLACK FACTS AT-A-GLANCE

1. January 15, 1929 Martin Luther King, Jr's Birthday.

2. Congress passes 13th Amendment which, on ratification, abolished slavery in America, January 24, 1865.

3. First Black U.S. Army regiment organized January 25, 1863.

4. January 31, 1962, Lt. Comdr. Samuel L. Gravely, became the first Black to command a U.S. Warship.

5. Ernest E. Just, Black biologist, received Spingarn Medal for pioneer research on fertilization and cell division, February 2, 1915.

6. The first Black student to be enrolled at University of Alabama, was Autherine Lucy, February 3, 1956.

7. Ragtime pianist and composer, Eubie Blake was born Feburary 7, 1883.

8. February 27, 1853, the first Black Y.M.C.A. was organized in Washington, D.C.

9. February 23, 1979, Frank E. Peterson, Jr. became the first Black general in the Marine Corps.

10. March 2, 1807 Congress banned the slave trade.

11 Jean Baptiste Pointe Du Sable, Black pioneer, founded Chicago March 13, 1773.

12 The first Black newspaper, Freedom's Journal, was published in New York City March 16, 1827.

13 Martin Luther King Jr., led thousands of marchers from Selma-to-Montgomery, Alabama, March 21, 1965.

14 March 26, 1911, William H. Lewis became assistant attorney general of the United States.

15 March 31, 1870, Thomas Peterson became the first Black to vote in the United States, after the 15th Amendment ratification.

16 Hank Aaron hit his 715th home run, breaking Babe Ruth's Major League baseball record, on April 8, 1974.

17 James B. Parsons, became the first Black Chief Judge of the Federal District Court in Chicago, April 18, 1975.

18 April 15, 1896, Booker T. Washington received honorary degree from Harvard University.

19 Emmett Ashford became the first Black Major League, umpire, April 12, 1966.

20 April 20, 1866 Fisk University opened in Nashville, Tenn.

21 April 21, 1565, Black explorers accompanied Menendez when St. Augustine, Fla. was founded.

22 Harold Washington was sworn in as Chicago's first Black Mayor, April 29, 1983.

23 May 5, 1950, Gwendolyn Brooks wins the Pulitzer Prize for poetry, "Annie Allen".

24 The first Black chaplain in the U.S. Army, Henry McNeal Turner, died May 8, 1915.

25 May 9, 1899, A.J. Burr patented the lawn mower.

26 Lincoln University, the first Black college, was founded May 24, 1054.

27 June 1, 1843, Sojourner Truth left New York and began a career as antislavery activist.

28 Wesley A. Brown became the first Black to graduate from Annapolis Academy, June 3, 1949.

29 June 13, 1967 Thurgood Marshall was appointed to the United States Supreme Court by President Johnson.

30 James Augustine, the first Black American Roman Catholic Bishop, was ordained June 10, 1854.

31 June 15, 1877, Henry O. Flipper became the first Black to graduate from West Point.

32 Arthur Ashe, Jr. won the men's Wimbledon singles Championship, July 5, 1975.

33 July 13, 1965, Thurgood Marshall was appointed first Black Solicitor General of the United States.

34 Violette A. Johnson, became the first Black woman to practice before the United States Supreme Court.

35 Jane Bolin became the first Black woman Judge in the United States, July 22, 1939.

36 The first Black Baptist Church in America was organized by eight slaves at Silver Bluff, S.C., July 25, 1777.

37 July 31, 1874, Patrick Francis Healy, was inaugurated as president of Georgetown University, Washington, D.C.

38 Matthew A. Henson, discoverer of the North Pole, was born August 8, 1865.

39 Ralph J. Bunche was named undersecretary of the United Nations, August 19, 1954.

40 Lt. Col. Guion S. Bluford, Jr., became the first Black astronaut, August 20, 1983.

41 Hiram B. Revels, the first Black U.S. Senator was born September 1, 1822.

42 John S. Durham, was named minister to Haiti, September 3, 1891.

43 F.W. Leslie patented envelope seal, September 21, 1897.

44 Vanessa Williams became the first Black, Miss America, September 17, 1983.

45 Constance Baker Motley, the first Black woman Federal Judge, was born September 14, 1921.

46 September 19, 1893, E.R. Robinson patented the Electric Railway Trolley.

47 September 9, 1960, Arthur Ashe, Jr. became the first Black tennis player to win the U.S. Open.

48 The first Black radio station, WERD, opened in Atlanta, October 3, 1949.

49 October 10, 1899, I.R. Johnson Patented the Bicycle Frame.

50 The first Black daily newspaper, the New Orleans Tribune, was founded October 4, 1864.

51 A. Miles patented the Elevator, October 11, 1887.

52 Martin Luther King Jr., won the Nobel Peace Prize, October 14, 1964.

53 Bishop Desmond Tutu won the Nobel Peace Prize, October 16, 1984.

54 The first Black bank, Capital Savings Bank Of Washington, D.C. opened October 17, 1888.

55 Omega Psi Phi Fraternity founded at Howard University October 28, 1914.

56 Richard Arrington was elected the first Black Mayor of Birmingham, Ala., October 30, 1979.

57 November 8, 1966, Edward W. Brooke became the first Black U.S. Senator since Reconstruction.

58 Andrew Hatcher was named associate press secretary to President John F. Kennedy, November 10, 1960.

59 Garrett A. Morgan, patened the Traffic Light, November, 20 1923.

60 Frederick Douglass published the first issue of the North Star Newspaper, December 3, 1847.

61 Poet, Phillis Wheatley died December 5, 1784.

62 Dr. Ralph J. Bunche, was the first Black to be awarded the Nobel Peace Prize, December 10, 1950.

63 Andrew Young became U.S. Delegate to the United Nation, December 16, 1976.

64 Rev. Jesse Jackson founded People United To Save Humanity, (PUSH) December 18, 1971.

ANSWERS

*1) Black Jockeys Who Won The Kentucky Derby—1. Oliver Lewis. 2. Billy Walker. 3. Barrett Lewis. 4. Babe Hurd. 5. Isaac Murphy. 6. Erskin Henderson 7. Isaac Lewis 8. Isaac Murphy 9. Isaac Murphy 10. Alonzo Clayton 11. James Perkins 12 Willie Sims 13 Willie Sims 14. Jimmy Winkfield. 15. Jimmy Winkfield.

*2) Groups; Who Sang That Song—1. (3). 2. (4). 3. (10). 4. (1). 5. (2). 6. (11). 7. (12). 8. (13). 9. (14). 10. (15). 11. (9). 12. (8). 13. (7). 14 (6). 15. (5).

*3) The Black Screen—1. Buck and The Preacher 2. Save The Children. 3. Blazing Saddles. 4. Three Tough Guys. 5. Mr. T. 6. Diana Ross. 7. Billy Dee Williams. 8. Sidney Poitier. 9. The Greatest. 10. Lou Gossett Jr. 11. Carmen Jones. 12. Cabin in The Sky 13. James Earl Jones 14 St. Louis Blues 15. The March of The Hawk. 16. If He Hollers, Let Him Go. 17. Melvin Van Peebles. 18. To Sir With Love. 19. Lady Sings The Blues. 21. Richard Pryor. 22. Billie Holiday 23. Pearl Bailey 24. Sounder. 25. Richard Pryor.

*6) Major Events in Black History: 1538-1983—1. 25th. 2. John H. Johnson. 3. Hazel Johnson 4. George E. Carruthers 5. Jesse Jackson 6. Thurgood Marshall. 7. Dr. Daniel H. Williams. 8. Shoe-making industry. 9. Emmett Ashford. 10. Diana Ross. 11. Corn planting machine. 12. Lee Elder. 13. Baseball team. 14. Harry McAlpin. 15. May, 1946. 16. Washington, D.C. 17. Eddie Robinson 18 Jane Matilda Bolin 19 William Du Bois 20. Percy Julian. 21. Brown v. Board of Education. 22. Wyandank. 23. Jesse Leroy Brown. 24. Charlotte E. Roy. 25. Constance Baker Motley. 26. Booker T. Washington. 27. Jenny Coupler. 28. Garrett Morgan. 29. Dr. Charles R. Drew. 30. Wilma Rudolph. 31. Althea Gibson. 32. South Carolina. 33. 25,000. 34. Lt. Comdr. Samuel L. Gravely. 35. New Mexico. 36. January 30, 1844. 37. Adam Clayton Powell Jr. 38. Crystal Bird Fauset. 39. Rev. Patrick Francis Healy S.J., PhD 40. New York City, March 16, 1827 41. Franklin County, Virginia 42. 1794. 43. July 2, 1964 44. Gene Mitchell Gray 45. Charlie Sifford. 46. J. T. Shutten. 47. Leonard Roy Harmon. 48. Henry McNeal Turner. 49. Julian Bond. 50. Lena Walker.

*12) Black Women in Music; Who Sang That Song—1. (7). 2. (6). 3. (1). 4. (10). 5. (9). 6. (8). 7. (4). 8. (3). 9. (5). 10. (2).

*13) Black Inventors and Scientists—1. (1). 2. (13). 3. (14). 4. (8). 5.(5) 6. (11). 7. (12). 8. (9). 9. (15). 10. (3). 11. (10). 12. (7). 13. (4). 14. (6). 15. (2).

*14) The Sports Scene # 1—1. Archie Moore. 2. Joe Frazier. 3. Arthur Ashe. 4. Wilt Chamberlain. 5. Muhammad Ali. 6. Cassius Clay. 7. Reggie Jackson. 8. Muhammad Ali 9. Sonny Liston 10. Hank Aaron. 11. Jesse Owens 12. Muhammad Ali 13. Joe Frazier 14. Jim Brown. 15. O.J. Simpson 16. Archie Moore 17. March 1, 1949. 18. 11 years 8 mos. 19. Maury Wills. 20. 1958 and 1959. 21. Wilma Rudolph 22. 1951, 1953 and 1955. 23 Sugar Ray Leonard 24. Julius Erving-Dr. J 25. Akeem Abdul Olajuwon.

*17) The Jazz Scene # 1—1. Electric Keyboard. 2. Trumpet. 3. Drums 4. Organ. 5. Saxophone. 6. Trumpet. 7. Drums 8. Trumpet 9. Tenor sax 10. Tenor sax. 11. Trumpet. 12. Bass. 13. Trumpet 14. Alto sax. 15. Guitar. 16. Piano. 17. Bass . 18. Saxophone. 19. Tenor sax. 20. Tenor sax. 21. Organ. 22. Fluegel horn. 23. Drums. 24. Alto sax. 25. Piano.

*19) Black First # 1—1. James Derham. 2. Oliver Lewis 3. Nicholas Biddle. 4. Macon B. Allen. 5. William Tucker 6. John Russwurm. 7. John H. Conyers. 8. Henry O. Flipper. 9. Moses Fleetwood Walker. 10. Harvard 1859-1871 11. West Point, June 15, 1877. 12. Louisiana. 13. 757,000. 14 Jonathan Jasper Wright 15. Island Mound, Missouri 16. Frank Thompson. 17. Charles Lewis Mitchell, Edward Garrison Walker. 18. Bishop Benjamin William Arnett 19. George Washington Carver 20. Dr. Rebecca Cole. 21. John Roy Lynch. 22. Georgia Infirmary 1832. 23. South Carolina 1526. 24. Boston 1891. 25. Liberia. 26. Richard Theodore Greener. 27. USS Marblehead. 28. Isabella Baumfree. 29. Oscar J. Dunn. 30. Alex ander Lucius Twilight. 31. Nathaniel Turner. 32. Dr. A.T. Angusta 33. Rev. Henry Highland Garnet 34. Jean Baptiste Pointe 35. Lemuel Haynes. 36. John Morront. 37. Sgt. William H. Carney. 38. Phillis Wheatley 39. Robert S. Duncanson. 40. J.T. Shutten. 41. W.W. Brown. 42. M.W. Gibbs. 43. Booker T. Washington. 44. Patricia R. Harris. 45. Henry Blair. 46. Marian Anderson. 47. Biddle College, Livingstone College, Biddle won 4-0. 48. Colored America. 49. Mary Patterson. 50. Associated Negro Press.

*25) True or False; Music—1. True. 2. False. (Impressions). 3. True. 4. True. 5. True. 6. True. 7. False. (Martha & The Vandellas). 8. True. 9. False. (Herbie Hancock). 10. True. 11. True. 12. True. 13. False. (1976). 14. True. 15. True.

*27) Black First # 2—1. Shirley Chisholm. 2. William H. Hastie. 3. Benjamin Oliver Davis Sr. 4. James A. Healy. 5. Madame C.J. Walker. 6. Daniel "Chappie" James. 7. Cheryl Adrenne Browne. 8. Benjamin Banneker. 9. Booker T. Washington. 10. Martin Luther King Jr. 11. Phyllis Mae Dolly. 12. Violette M. Anderson. 13. Edward Thomas Demley. 14. Chris Dickerson. 15. Frank Robinson. 16. Jessie Owens 17. Irving Charles Mollison. 18. Frances E.W. Harper. 19. John Earl Rudder. 20. Richard Allen. 21. Willie Mays. 22. Lee Elder 23. Prairie View Bowl 24. Fritz Pollard 25. Jackie Robinson (1949) 26. Dan Bankhead 27 Leroy Satchell Paige 28 Egbert (Bert) Williams 29. Bill Cosby 30. Hattie McDaniel. 31. Alice Walker. 32. Sidney Poitier. 33. Adam Wade. 34. Hearts in Dixie. 35. Henry Lewis. 36. Janet Collins. 37. Renard Edwards 38. Billy Dee Williams 39. Sidney Poitier 40. Beverly Johnson. 41. Alpha Kappa Alpha. 42. North Star. 43. Hiram Rhodes Revels. 44. Blanche K. Bruce. 45. New Orleans Tribune. 46. Roscoe Robinson Jr. 47. Joseph L. Searles III. 48. Charles S. Johnson. 49. Ralph Bunche. 50. Wesley A. Brown.

*32) Jazz Scene # 2—1. Saxophone. 2. Electric Keyboard. 3. Piano. 4. Banjo, guitar. 5. Banjo, guitar. 6. Bass. 7. Saxophone. 8. Trumpet. 9. Drums 10. Trombone 11. Drums 12. Trumpet 13. Clarinet 14. Drums 15. Trombone. 16. Trombone. 17. Guitar. 18. Bass. 19. Trumpet. 20. Piano. 21. Bass 22. Trumpet 23. Clarinet 24. Trombone 25. Trumpet.

*34) Rhythm and Blues; Who Sang That Song—1. Michael Jackson. 2. Curtis Mayfield. 3. Ohio Players. 4. Temptations. 5. Stevie Wonder. 6. Eddie Kendricks. 7. Chuck Berry. 8. Jerry Butler. 9. Isaac Hayes. 10. O'Jays.

*35) The Sports Scene # 2—1. (a). 2. (c). 3. (a). 4. (b). 5. (b). 6. (a). 7. (a). 8. (b). 9. (a). 10. (a).

*37) Real Names—1. Isabella Baumfree. 2. Walker Smith Jr. 3. Ray Charles Robinson. 4. Michael Luther King. 5. Riley B. King. 6. Loretta Mary Aiken. 7. Lawrence Tero. 8. Cassius Clay. 9. Ferdinand Lewis Alcindor Jr 10 Ernest Evans 11 Robert Calvin Bland 12. Charles Edward Anderson Berry. 13. Steveland Morris. 14. William Edward Burgharat DuBois. 15. Joseph Louis Barrow.

*38) Black Heritage Stamps—1. February 1, 1984. 2. February 4, 1986. 3. March 5, 1985. 4. February 15, 1980. 5. Janurary 13, 1979. 6. February 1, 1978. 7. February 20, 1987 8. August 2, 1982 9. Janurary 30, 1981. 10. February 2, 1988. 11. June 9, 1983. 12. February 1, 1990. 13. February 3, 1989.

*45) Black Congressmen of the Past—1. Blanche K. Bruce. 2. John A. Hyman. 3. Jeremiah Haralson. 4. Arthur W. Mitchell 5. Hiram Rhodes Revels. 6. Joseph H. Rainey 7. John R. Lynch 8. Charles E. Nash. 9. Robert C. Delarge 10. Oscar De Priest 11. Richard H. Cain 12. Henry P. Cheatham 13. George W. Collins 14. William L. Dawson 15. Adam Clayton Powell Jr.

*49) Identify the Group—1. Rufus. 2. Spinners. 3. The Commodores. 4. Earth, Wind and Fire. 5. The Temptations. 6. The Temptations. 7. The Impressions. 8. Supremes. 9. The Temptations. 10. The Miracles. 11. The Blue Notes. 12. The Temptations 13. The Jackson 5. 14. Drifter's 15. Bob Marley & The Wailers.

*50) Major Events in Black History # 2 1775- 1983—1. True. 2. True. 3. True. 4. True. 5. True. 6. False. (2254). 7. False (1894). 8. False. (Louisiana). 9. True. 10. True. 11. True. 12. False. (1887). 13. True 14. True. 15. True.

*52) Black First # 3 —1. (c). 2. (a). 3. (c). 4. (b). 5. (c). 6. (a). 7. (a). 8. (a). 9. (a). 10. (a). 11. (a). 12. (c).

*54) Nicknames; Sports—1. (3). 2. (5). 3. (6). 4. (7). 5. (8). 6. (4). 7. (1). 8. (9). 9. (2). 10. (11). 11. (12). 12. (10). 13. (15). 14. (13). 15. (14).

*55) Rhythm and Blues; Who Sang That Song # 2—1. (7). 2. (2) 3. (9). 4. (12). 5. (1). 6. (14). 7. (11). 8. (3). 9. (13). 10. (8). 11. (5). 12. (15) 13. (6). 14. (10). 15. (4).

*56) Inventions by Blacks; 1834-1960—1. Wade Washington. 2. Grainville T. Woods. 3. Grainville T. Woods. 4. Lewis Temple. 5. Henry Blair. 6. Frederick M. Jones. 7. Frederick M. Jones. 8. Jan Matzeliger 9. Lewis Howard Latimer. 10. Norbert Rillieux 11. Grainville T. Woods. 12. S.R. Scottron. 13. Joseph H. Smith 14. Andrew J. Beard 15. Charles B. Brooks. 16. Sarah Boone. 17. O.E. Brown 18. Henry Blair 19. A.L. Cralle. 20. George F. Grant. 21. B.F. Jackson. 22. Frederick M. Jones 23. Frederick M. Jones 24. R.B. Spikes 25. J.W. West. 26. R.J Winters. 27. T.W. Stewart 28. P.D. Smith 29. Frederick M. Jones 30. Leonard C. Bailey 31 John Lee Love 32. A. Miles 33. Albert A. Jones, Amos E. Long. 34. Latimer and Nichols. 35. Elijah McCoy. 36. Elijah McCoy. 37. O'Conner and Turner. 38. William B. Purvis. 39. Willis Johnson. 40. John Lee Love. 41. W.R. Davis. 42. William Bailes. 43. A.B. Blackburn. 44. A.B. Blackburn. 45. I.R. Johnson. 46. George Carruthers 47. W.A. Martin. 48. L. Bell. 49. J.A. Burr. 50. J.W. Butts.

*63) Black Writers—1. Lerone Bennett Jr. 2. Arna Bontemps. 3. Ed Bullins. 4. Margaret Walker 5. Charles Waddell Chesnutt. 6. Paul Laurence. Dunbar. 7. Nikki Giovanni. 8. John Edgar Wideman. 9. Chester Himes.

*65) Black Mayors; Past and Present—1. Walter E. Washington. 2. Ernest N. Morial. 3. Birmingham. 4. Chicago. 5. W. Wilson Goode. 6. Andrew Young 7. Richmond 8. Thomas Bradley 9. Coleman Young 10. Atlanta 11. Tuskegee, Ala. 12. A.J. Cooper. 13. Kenneth A. Gibson. 14. Gary, Indiana. 15. Carl B. Stokes, Cleveland, Ohio.

*67) Black Cowboys—1. Crawford Goldsby. 2. Daniel Webster Wallace. 3. Bill Pickett. 4. Ned Huddleston. 5. Nat Love.

*72) Historic Landmarks of Black Americans—1. Oakland Memorial Chapel, Alcorn University. 2. Old Fort Grant, Bonita ,Arizona. 3. Mary McLeod Bethune Memorial, District of Columbia. 4. Mary Ann Shadd Cary House District of Columbia. 5. Henry O. Tanner Homesite, Philadelphia, Penn. 6. The Battle of Rhode Island. 7. Jean Baptiste Pointe Du Sable Homesite, Chicago, Illinois. 8. John Roosevelt "Jackie" Robinson Residence. 9. Claude McKay Residence. 10. Maggie Lena Walker House. 11. Charles Richard Drew House. 12. South View Cemetery, Atlanta, Georgia. 13.Tuskegee Institute, Tuskegee, Alabama 14. Howard University, District of Columbia. 15. Booker T. Washington, New York City. 16. Blanche K. Bruce House, District of Columbia. 17. Provident Hospital and Training School, Chicago, Illinois 18. Bethune-Cookman College, Daytona Beach, Florida 19. Ralph Bunche House, Queens, New York. 20. Sierra Nevada.

*81) Black Quotations—1. (a). 2. (b). 3. (a). 4. (c). 5. (a). 6. (c). 7. (c). 8. (a). 9. (d). 10. (a). 11. (b). 12. (b). 13. (a). 14. (c). 15. (b).

*84) Black Women—1. Crystal Bird Fauset. 2. Bessie Coleman. 3. Mary McLeod Bethune. 4. Dr. Ida Gray 5. Charlotta A. Bass. 6. Madame C.J. Walker. 7. Dorothy B. Ferebee. 8. Mary Ann Shadd Cary.

*87) Rhythm and Blues; Who Sang That Song—1. (c). 2. (d). 3. (a). 4. (c). 5. (a). 6. (d) 7. (a). 8. (b). 9. (a). 10. (a). 11. (a). 12. (a). 13. (b). 14. (d). 15. (a).

*90) Some Who Made A Difference—1. Diamond Grove, Missouri. 2. Spelman College. 3. George Washington Carver. 4. Taliaferro. 5. Booker T. Washington. 6. Harriet Tubman 7. Ralph J. Bunche 8. Marian Anderson. 9. James Meredith. 10. Vivian Malone. 11. Robert C. Weaver. 12. Bill Russell. 13. A.J. Cooper 14. April 4, 1968. 15. (6) 16. John Lee Hooker 17. W.C. Handy. 18. Ellicott, Maryland. 19. George Washington Carver. 20. True. 21. True. 22. Diana Ross. 23. Mobile, Alabama. 24. True. 25. Booker T. Washington. 26. Marcus Garvey. 27. Whitney Young 28. Jean Baptiste Pointe De Sable. 29. 3 times. 30. True. 31. True. 32. Floyd Patterson. 33. Archie Moore. 34. True. 35. Sidney Poitier. 36. True. 37. Bill Cosby. 38. Gone With The Wind. 39. Sammy Davis Jr. 40. Carter G. Woodson. 41. True. 42. True. 43. Benjamin Oliver Davis Jr. 44. Congressman William L. Dawson. 45. Ralph J. Bunche. 46. Andrew Hatcher. 47. Martin Luther King Jr 48. Martin Luther King Jr 49. William H. Hastie. 50. Andrew F. Brimmer. 51. Hattie McDaniel 52. Juan De Pareja. 53. Dr. Percy Julian 54. Muhammad Ali 55. True 56. True 57. Mose Fleetwood. 58. Benjamin Bannaker. 59. Henry Armstrong 60. Whitney Moore Young. 61. True. 62. True. 63. Gwendolyn Brooks. 64. John Thompson. 65. E. Frederic Morrow. 66. Harriet Tubman. 67. Marcus Garvey. 68. United States Colored Troops. 69. Bill Cosby. 70. Atlanta Stadium. 71. Arthur Dovington. 72. Maj. Frederick D. Gregory, Maj. Guion S. Bluford, Dr. Ronald E. McNail 73. Clara Brown 74. Mary McLeod Bethune 75. Harriet Tubman.

*98) Who Sang That Song "Sixties"—1. The Platters 2. Fats Domino 3. Bill Cosby 4. The Marvelettes 5. Junior Walker & The All Stars 6. Ray Charles 7. Sly & The Family Stone 8 Sam Cooke 9. The Crystals 10. Hank Ballard

*99) The Black Screen— 1. Uptown Saturday Night. 2. Amazing Grace. 3. Mahogany. 4. Cat Ballou. 5. A Man Called Adam. 6. Slaves. 7. The Informer. 8. Martin Luther King; The Man and The March. 9. The Man. 10. California Suite. 11. Greased Lighting. 12. Mother, Jugs and Speed. 13. Scott Joplin. 14. Bingo Long and The Traveling All-Stars and Motor Kings 15. Shaft. 16. Sugar Hill. 17. Norman, Is That You. 18. Jimmy Cliff. 19. Book of Numbers. 20. Which Way Is Up.

*103) Black Facts At-a-Glance